How Latin America Views the U. S. Investor

PRAEGER SPECIAL STUDIES IN
INTERNATIONAL ECONOMICS AND DEVELOPMENT

How Latin America Views the U. S. Investor

Edited by

Raymond Vernon

Published in cooperation with
the Harvard University
Graduate School of Business Administration

FREDERICK A. PRAEGER, Publishers
New York · Washington · London

The purpose of the Praeger Special Studies is to make specialized research monographs in international economics and politics available to the academic, business, and government communities. For further information, write to the Special Projects Division, Frederick A. Praeger, Publishers, 111 Fourth Avenue, New York, N.Y. 10003.

FREDERICK A. PRAEGER, PUBLISHERS
111 Fourth Avenue, New York, N.Y. 10003, U.S.A.
77-79 Charlotte Street, London, W.1, England

Published in the United States of America in 1966
by Frederick A. Praeger, Inc., Publishers

Library of Congress Catalog Card Number: 65-24704

Printed in the United States of America

FOREWORD

"O wad some Power the giftie gie us
to see oursels as ithers see us!
It wad frae mony a blunder free us,
an foolish notion:..."

... Robert Burns

Although this is a book about the Latin American
view of the United States investor, its inspiration
clearly springs from the Scots. What it tries to
achieve is what Robbie Burns thought to be so difficult: to see ourselves, even if just for a moment,
through the eyes of the dyspeptic outsider.

The United States investor with an interest in
Latin America rarely has the opportunity to see himself through Latin eyes. For one thing, those with
whom he has contact in Latin America may see little
advantage and considerable risk in utter frankness.
For another thing, the investor's antennae may not
be attuned to receiving the subtle signals which are
being broadcast.

To see ourselves as others see us is not necessarily to see an undistorted image. Latin Americans
cannot fail to view United States investors through
an historical haze made up of the Monroe Doctrine,
the marine landings at Vera Cruz and Santo Domingo,
the riots in the Canal Zone, and the quotas on sugar
imports. They interpret what they see through a
cultural prism shaped by such forces as their His-
panic origins, Napoleonic law, Indian culture, and
the trials and tribulations of underdevelopment.

It is scarcely surprising, therefore, that
some of the interpretations contained in my colleagues' essays in this little volume are at variance with my own views. As I prepared the manuscripts

for publication, I found myself seized from time to time with the urge to drop one of those "yes, but..." notes with which editors sometimes betray their authors. But I resolutely stifled the urge whenever it arose, thereby keeping faith both with the authors and with the readers.

For who can say what "objective reality" is? Who can be certain that the Latin American does not see us in a more dispassionate light than we see ourselves? Besides, it is quite unimportant, for the limited purposes of this book, whether my colleagues' views conform to "objective reality," whatever that is. Their views, objective or not, may move mountains; or if not that, may at least start or stop revolutions.

The papers collected together in this little volume were the result of a project organized under the George H. Leatherbee Lecture Fund at the Harvard Business School in the Spring of 1965. Those by Jaguaribe and Vernon were presented publicly on May 18. The Garcia Vazquez paper never saw the light of day; as Vice President of the Argentine central bank, he found himself pinned down in Buenos Aires on the day scheduled for its delivery. Wionczek's appearance at Harvard was also prevented at the last moment, as a result of a tragic illness in the family.

Taken together, the four papers offer a picture derived from a variety of viewpoints. The variety springs partly from the differences in coverage of the various papers, partly from the differences in the identity of the authors. Collectively, however, they reflect the views of a major, influential sector of Latin American life.

The authors themselves guarantee a certain variety. The Garcia Vazquez paper comes from the pen of an Argentine official, restrained by public responsibility, propelled by a desire to put his country in a favorable light, yet desirous also of putting the investor on notice of his responsibilities as well as his opportunities. The Jaguaribe paper represents the view of a political scientist and former government official, an academic now without official responsibility. Wionczek's paper is the product of a naturalized Mexican, well known for his scholarship in Latin American affairs, involved while at the same time detached in his judgments of Latin American behavior. My own contribution claims a place in this collection only tenuously; my past research on the economy of Mexico may give me the right to speak of the Mexican view, though the view is obviously more vicarious than that of my colleagues.

Nonetheless, despite the diversities of viewpoint, there is a thread of agreement in all the four papers. To understand the Latin American view, the United States investor will have to be prepared to hear a challenge to some of his more cherished preconceptions: his view of the "right" role of the private and the public sector; his view of the economic consequences of foreign investment; his view of the common area of interest between himself and local private entrepreneurs. The experience may be painful; but, if Robbie Burns is to be believed, it may be worth the pain.

Raymond Vernon
Professor of International
  Trade and Investment
Harvard Business School

Boston, Massachusetts

August, 1965

CONTENTS

LIST OF TABLES

A LATIN AMERICAN VIEW

by

Miguel S. Wionczek

> Nationalism, which is pre-eminently
> a state of mind rather than a state of
> nature, has become a dominant and uni-
> versal state of mind in the twentieth
> century.
>
> J. W. Fulbright, <u>Old Myths</u>
> <u>and New Realities</u>

Benjamin Higgins once said that the road to economic development is paved with vicious circles. Nowhere is the validity of this statement more obvious
than in the participation of foreign private investment in Latin American development.

Latin America faces unfavorable prospects for
international primary commodity trade, a relatively
low level of domestic savings, demographic pressures
on available resources, and a rapidly increasing
cost of modern technology. As a result, most development experts agree that Latin America must receive
significant amounts of foreign private capital if it
is to achieve sustained economic growth during the
next two decades. At the same time, however, private capital flows from industrial countries, present
and anticipated, are looked upon with very serious
apprehension by large sectors of the Latin American
public. Hostile attitudes toward foreign private

Miguel S. Wionczek is Adviser, Center for Latin
American Monetary Studies in Mexico City.

capital (and especially toward United States private
capital) are present in varying degrees in practically all Latin American republics. During the most
recent years, this hostility has been gathering con-
tinuously in strength--this, in spite of the fact
that the present inflow of foreign private capital
to the area represents probably only one third of
the total foreign financial resources made available
to Latin America by capital exporting countries.

     To an outside observer, this hostility may seem
to be out of proportion to the actual or potential
role of foreign-owned or foreign-controlled corporations in most Latin American economies. Rough estimates of the book value of foreign private direct
investment in the region in 1964 placed it at about
$14,500 million, or considerably less than in either
Canada or Western Europe. Out of this total, about
35% is located in Venezuela, mainly in petroleum;
another 35% in three major countries (Argentina,
Brazil and Mexico); some 10% in Peru and Colombia;
and the rest in a dozen smaller republics. In no
Latin American republic does foreign investment, including the reinvestment of profits of already established firms, approach 10% of the gross fixed investment; on the average for the area, foreign investment
comes to only about 6% of total investment. Having
in mind the need to achieve an annual per capita income increase on the order of 2.5 or 3.0% during the
next decade, experts from the Inter-American Alliance
for Progress Committee have recently estimated the
foreign private long-term capital necessities for
Latin America at an average of $550 millions a year.[1]
A leading Mexican economist has produced an even lower estimate, between $400 and $500 millions annually.[2]

     Obviously it is not the absolute magnitude of
the foreign private direct investment in the region,
either present or prospective, which explains the
widespread negative attitude toward foreign-controlled
enterprises in Latin America. Part of the reason for
the rejection of the foreign private enterprise as
one of the principal engines of development in Latin
America stems from a preoccupation with the possible
long-run negative impact of large-scale foreign

investment on the area's precarious balance of payments position. But essentially, this hostility involves much deeper, much less tangible issues.

The hostility toward foreign private investment
reflects, on the one hand, a strong desire of the
new elites of Latin America to achieve real political
and economic independence from the advanced industrial Western countries, which they blame for the
region's past and present backwardness.[3] At the
same time, ironically enough, the modernizing impact
of foreign investment feeds the fears of powerful
traditional groups whose privileged economic status
is being endangered by the modernizing process in
Latin American societies. That deep conflict exists
between Latin American societies and foreign investors, therefore, no one should doubt.

To begin with, I propose to look more closely
at the nature of the conflict. Then, the conflict
will be analyzed as it arises in the framework of
the area's various regional economic integration pro-
grams--notably the Latin American Free Trade Area
and the Central American Common Market.

THE NATURE OF THE CONFLICT

Voluminous records of hearings held in the past
few years before the United States Congress and frequent declarations by private business organizations
in the United States and elsewhere suggest that foreign sources of private capital have a view of Latin
America bearing a most tenuous relationship to reality. This view is composed of various stereotypes,
built around a general idea of a world divided into
a free zone of free enterprise and a captive zone of
"socialistic" societies.

Thinking in an ideological framework, Latin
America is seen as one of the main targets of a "com-
munist offensive," whether of Castroist, Soviet or
Chinese type. One of the principal objectives of
this offensive is to sow hatred against foreign private enterprise, and to create political and psycho-

logical conditions which would ease the way to take-
overs of foreign-held properties by communist-type
regimes based on local or on international conspira-
cies.

According to this line of thought, the present
disappointing state of the Latin American economies
is largely due to a lack of appreciation of the potential role of the private enterprise, whether
domestic or foreign. Private enterprise is seen as
the most important single developmental factor; if
left to itself, private enterprise would bring rapid
economic development, would increase social welfare,
and would lay the groundwork for a sound and stable
political democracy.

In addition, there are intimations, especially
in the United States, of some kind of conspiracy between the mistaken or perverse Latin American intellectual elites, deeply committed to statist tendencies, and the allegedly inefficient bureaucracies in
the developed countries which administer governmental
aid programs. These groups are said to operate from
a common conviction that development must be largely
promoted by the state. They are held responsible
for channelling foreign aid and assistance to Latin
America through governments, instead of fostering
the flow of private capital to Latin America and the
withdrawal of official aid as rapidly as possible.
Under such adverse conditions, private enterprise is
said to be unable to contribute fully to the rapid
and efficient achievement of economic growth and political democracy in the Southern part of the Western
Hemisphere.

This diagnosis leads to the claim that foreign
private investment should receive all possible guarantees both from the capital-exporting and the capital-
receiving nations in order to offset the growing investment risks in the area and in order to provide
profits commensurate with the existing risks.

Such an image of Latin America and the difficulties facing foreign capital in the area is deeply imprinted in the majority of leading corporate minds,

and is reinforced by frequent declarations not only
from spokesmen for business groups but also from political figures in the industrial countries. The
following excerpt from a report of a United States
Congressional sub-committee is characteristic of many:

> North Americans (and West Europeans, as
> well) who live under and enjoy the benefits
> of a predominantly free enterprise, private-
> investment market system of economic organi-
> zation are increasingly concerned about the
> lagging role of private investment in the
> Latin American development program. They
> are concerned also with the attitude of seem-
> ing indifference in many parts of Latin Amer-
> ica itself to the potential contributions of
> the private sector. This local apathy is
> manifest in a concentration of energies on
> governmental development programs, the re-
> ported exodus of domestic capital, the
> flight from foreign currencies and the per-
> sistent discouragement which private, and
> especially foreign private, capital seem-
> ingly must face.[4]

A characteristic apologia for the role of private enterprise is reflected in the following pas-
sages from another source:

> . . . private enterprises (anywhere in the
> world) are responsive and accountable to
> the will and interest of the people in four
> ways: to public opinion, as expressed in
> representative government and a free press
> and other media of mass communications; to
> the law, as embodied in legislation and
> government regulations affecting private
> economic behavior; to the discipline of
> the competitive market, which reflects the
> preferences and choices of the people act-
> ing as consumers, wage earners, stockhold-
> ers, and investors; and to the countervail-
> ing power of trade unions, organizations
> and farmers, and other enterprises oper-
> ating as competitors, suppliers and cus-

tomers. . . . The growth of modern private
enterprise would not by itself be sufficient to ensure greater welfare, justice,
and personal and political freedom for
Latin Americans, but it is one of the
essential conditions for achieving these
values.[5]

Convinced that private enterprise, whether do-
mestically or foreign owned, possesses an impressive
array of ethical, social and economic virtues, foreign business executives are puzzled by the fact
that the large majority of Latin Americans looks
with considerable suspicion at a private entrepreneur, and particularly at a foreign corporation.
That fact, however, is often explained by Latin
America's ignorance, as follows:

. . . neither capitalism, as a system in
which innovative management in the corporate form is extensively exploited, nor
socialism, in which state planning and public management is employed, is well understood by Latin Americans. The continuing
ideological controversy in Latin America
is not between the merit of present-day
capitalism as practiced in the United
States and Western Europe, versus socialism as practiced in Soviet Russia, but
rather it is between a concept of capitalism that had some similarity to reality 75
years ago, and a concept of socialism that
has never existed anywhere in practice.
. . . Likewise, the true character of
modern corporate enterprise and its international potential is poorly understood
in Latin America. There is no cause to
fear the political power of private enterprise today. Private business is society's
most ideologically neutral institution, its
most specifically goal-directed force.[6]

Latin Americans respond to all this by pointing
out, among other things, that they can hardly be
blamed for the lack of understanding of modern cap-

italism since they have not as yet been exposed to
it. An enlightened Latin American statesman, former
President of Colombia, Alberto Lleras Camargo, puts
it in these terms:

> Under the umbrella of capitalism and
> free enterprise, the United States has
> grown in power and justice. But in Latin
> America, the very same system not infre-
> quently has led to odious and infamous
> concentrations of capital and of means of
> production. This type of capitalism owns
> vast land areas--certainly the best land;
> it scarcely pays any taxes; it controls
> agricultural and industrial credit; and
> there is no law or power in the state that
> can stand against its monolithic advance.[7]

The political scientist or economic historian
has no difficulty in understanding why so many Latin
Americans--especially the younger generations whose
fathers migrated from the backward countryside or
came out of urban slums--show little appreciation
for the free enterprise system. Nor is the hostility of intellectuals, who play a much more important
role in transitional societies than in the opulent
industrial countries, a source of mystery. The
Latin American capitalism with which these groups
are acquainted is reminiscent, in many respects, of
the United States capitalism of the era of the
"Robber Barons," in the latter decades of the nineteenth century. It may be that foreign private capital adheres faithfully to the rules set by the backward social and political framework of the transitional societies; nevertheless, this is not enough
to distinguish it from the rest of the free enterprise sector. Accordingly, it is directly blamed
for all the shortcomings of that sector even if it
has long since changed the character of its own
performance.

A memory of history lingers much longer in the
transitional slowly changing societies than in the
dynamic advanced communities. Latin Americans cannot easily forget the experiences of the past few

generations; they remember the era when large foreign corporations solved their local problems with
the help of open political and even military intervention of the governments of great industrial powers. Much more recent developments, particularly
developments involving international petroleum and
mining companies operating in the region, make it
implausible for the average man on the streets of
Caracas, Lima or Buenos Aires to believe that foreign private capital is politically neutral and economically beneficial. It may be that companies such
as United Fruit are now paying wages higher than
domestic land-owners, are training local agricultural economists, and are selling some of their plantations to local farmers; but despite present policies, United Fruit continues to be a symbol of foreign penetration and exploitation in Central America.

All these factors explain why government after
government in Latin America, almost independently of
its political coloring, discourages the entry of new
foreign private capital and uses numerous legal
stratagems to diminish the relative role of existing
foreign direct investment in certain fields. Out-
right prohibitions are rare. But among the member
countries of the Latin American Free Trade Area
(LAFTA), which together account for some 80% of
Latin America's gross national product, the following branches of business are restricted in some way
to participation by foreign private capital: in
Argentina, petroleum; in Brazil, petroleum and mass
communications media; in Chile, petroleum, mining,
shipping and insurance; in Mexico, petroleum, mining,
public utilities, fisheries, forestry, heavy petrochemicals, banking, insurance, radio and motion pic-
tures; in Paraguay, petroleum and public utilities;
and in Peru, petroleum, insurance, air transport and
mass communications media. Only in a few Latin American Republics, notably Colombia, Ecuador, and Venezuela, can a prospective foreign investor find complete freedom of operation.

Few would deny that foreign capital has made a
contribution to the development of Latin America.
The exploitation of natural resources by foreign

capital, which began in post-colonial Latin America
about the middle of the nineteenth century, was followed shortly afterwards by the appearance of
foreign-controlled services supporting export activity; and then activities contributed to inward-
oriented economic growth in which local entrepreneurs
soon played an important role. Where incipient industrial activities already existed at the time of
the opening of the country to foreign capital, the
stimulating effect of such capital was significant.
In the smaller and politically weaker countries,
however, inward-looking growth scarcely took place
at all, and over a number of generations foreign
corporations made no effort to bring domestic capital and skill into what was considered highly profitable activities. Long before anyone had heard of
Fidel Castro, Latin American intellectuals and entrepreneurs had begun to look on foreign private investment in the traditional minerals-exploiting export-
oriented fields as retarding rather than fostering
economic and political growth. Only a few years ago,
a leading Latin American economist, Raul Prebisch,
had these harsh words to say about foreign private
capital invested in traditional operations in the
area:

> The social structure handed down from
> the times of the externally geared devel-
> opment was associated with the characteris-
> tic type of foreign investment aimed mainly
> at serving, in one way or another, the in-
> terests of the major centers of which the
> undertaking concerned were an offshoot.
> They continue essentially, now as then, to
> lean towards the development of mineral re-
> sources, export and allied activities, and
> public utility concessions. . . . They
> made no attempt to disseminate . . . [ad-
> vanced] techniques within the country, nor
> was there any reason for them to do so,
> since extensive farming of the land by the
> country's own population usually required
> no more than a rudimentary technology.
> Moreover, such private enterprise as
> emerged from time to time in our countries

to engage in activities similar to those
of the enclaves often ended in the domestic efforts being engulfed by them or dis-
appearing under their economic pressure.
. . . These enclaves of the past, which
are still with us, must either change by
themselves or give way to domestic enterprise. The days when foreign enterprise
came in to do what Latin America could not
do are definitely over. We need the outside world to help us to cultivate our own
ability, so that the population as a whole
can be brought to share in the process of
development.[8]

The rejection of the proposition that foreign
private capital should be regarded as a major developmental factor in Latin America reflects a widespread
feeling of frustration about the course and results
of the Latin American development under traditional
laissez-faire rules--rules which are still in force
as the basis of international economic relations.
This feeling of frustration is responsible for the
insistent emphasis since the mid-fifties on the ur-
gent need for regional economic cooperation. Such
cooperation would open a wide new market to weak domestic industries by offering them economies of scale
and external economies. At the same time, it would
strengthen Latin America's bargaining position vis-
à-vis the industrialized North. It may well be, as
many outside critics insist, that the rationale for
these regional programs of action is built around a
number of theoretically unproven assumptions. For
Latin Americans, however, the rationale is inherent-
ly logical and fully in accord with Latin American
reality, even if the diagnosis is partially intui-
tive.

For one and a half centuries after the achievement of political independence, Latin America main-
tained close economic relations with the advanced
countries; yet almost all of Latin America is still
far away from the stage of the take-off into self-
sustained growth. Distances between the average
levels of economic development and social welfare in

the advanced countries and Latin America are steadily increasing and the obstacles to growth are being
compounded by a demographic explosion for which the
scientific and technological advances in the developed countries are held largely responsible. Socio-
political tensions are building up in the midst of
antiquated political structures, which range from
repressive dictatorships to systems which masquerade
as representative democracies. Semi-feudal conditions persist in large parts of the countryside, and
lopsided industrial structures are artificially main-
tained within segmented national markets. The only
change that is really significant in recent years is
the spreading conviction that these conditions need
not continue forever.

Since the liberal economic policies followed
for many generations in Latin America brought few
widespread social and economic advances and since
the national economic development programs generated
during the past twenty years have run repeatedly
into blind alleys, the modernizing elements of Latin
American society have been searching for new solutions. Contrary to many outside opinions, these
solutions do not imply a complete break with past
economic policies. But they do aim at changing the
nature of traditional relationships between Latin
America and the rest of the world and at bringing
some element of rationality into Latin American economic policies. The efforts of foreign capital to
perpetuate the political and economic dependence of
Latin America on the industrial countries, particularly dependence on the United States, represents
probably the single most important element in the
growing conflict between foreign private capital and
Latin American societies. Latin America's new modern elites, weak though they may be, want in fact to
change the nature of capitalism as it has been known
in the area. Whether in the public or private sector, these modernizing elites want to substitute
regional interdependence for external dependence.
At the same time, they want to elaborate a new political and economic ideology suitable for the rapid
solution of the problem of economic and political
backwardness. In other words, the newly emerging

elites reject the continuation of Latin America's
role as an appendage to a world economy centered
around the North Atlantic. They do not want to be
treated as a source of cheap raw materials whose ex-
traction is based upon the abundance of cheap labor,
nor to be looked upon as a market for over-priced
manufactured goods. They refuse to serve as a target for the plans of foreign private capital, as
long as such capital insists on entering the region
only when privileged treatment is assured and complete freedom of action guaranteed.

Some might object that these views, so widely
accepted in Latin America, are a caricature of Latin
America's role in the world economy. But that is
the image imprinted in Latin American minds, nevertheless. The image lost some of its force during
the era of Franklin D. Roosevelt. This was because
of the enlightened U.S. policy in Latin America in
that period. Again during a year or two of the
Kennedy administration, the sharp edges of this image became somewhat blurred, when it appeared that a
sympathetic understanding of the nature of Latin
American problems once again had gained the upper
hand in Washington.[9] But after Kennedy's death,
Latin Americans once more saw themselves as the un-
derprivileged stepchildren of the advanced world,
due to ambivalent and contradictory policies followed in the region by the industrialized countries
and due to the return to Realpolitik in Washington.

Whatever their political allegiances may be,
Latin Americans resent the mounting offensive of
large foreign corporations--corporations mainly head-
quartered in the U.S.--for special privileges and
treatment in the capital receiving countries. This
offensive was visible in the recent development of a
Convention on the Settlement of Investment Disputes
to which all Latin American states objected. It
manifested itself in a similar draft convention on
the protection of foreign property, discussed for
some time within the OECD in Paris. It has been apparent in direct pressures put on Latin American
countries to sign bilateral foreign investment guarantee agreements under AID auspices, and in similar

actions aimed at giving foreign private investors a
special status in the capital receiving country. Ob-
jection is raised not only to giving special status
to foreign nationals and corporations in their disputes with sovereign states, but also to the basic
implication that the interests of foreign owners
should override the interests of a national state.[10]
On this point, an overwhelming majority of politically literate Latin Americans would subscribe to a
statement made recently not by a Latin American radical but by a conservative African banker:

> . . . we, too, need certain guarantees
> from you. This business of guarantees and
> assurances is a two-way street. The peo-
> ples in Africa have had and are still hav-
> ing unholy experiences with members of the
> free enterprise system--with members of
> capitalism--and therefore they are justi-
> fied in being fearful and in requiring
> certain guarantees from you.[11]

What are the sources of conflict between large
foreign corporations operating in Latin America and
the local societies in which they operate? As far
as Latin America itself is concerned, most of the
available literature on the subject, depending on
its source, is either pure hagiography of capitalist
exploits for the benefit of the humanity, or pure
nationalist propaganda.[12] Two sources of conflict,
however, arise repeatedly. One is based on the concern that foreign-controlled corporations will be
operated without regard to the national aspirations
and national interests of the host country. The
other is based on the fear that foreign owned industry may move in to take the lion's share of the
fruits of economic development in the form of profits.[13] Foreign-owned industrial enterprise has a
tremendous advantage over Latin American firms in
terms of financial power and technology. Restraints
upon the monopolistic tendencies of large foreign
firms in the form of anti-trust legislation hardly
exist in the region. And the secretiveness with
which foreign enterprises surround their operations
adds to the concern that their reach and their rewards may both be excessive.

Foreign-controlled companies complain that the Latin American public opinion has a grossly exaggerated view of their profits. Few people in the area, however, are ready to accept the validity of the official data, published by governments of capital exporting countries, which appear to show that the profit levels of companies operating overseas are roughly similar to that of the parent companies at home.[14]

The Latin American economist, politician or man of the street is aware that domestic industrialists as a rule make extremely handsome profits because of domestic protectionist policies, inter-company collusion, and tax evasion. They cannot accept the proposition that the foreign entrepreneur, endowed with access to modern technology, good management techniques, abundant capital funds and high bargaining power vis-à-vis host governments, could be earning less than his weaker national counterpart. In the opinion of many Latin Americans, foreign-owned enterprises must be making full use of all the legal devices available in order to declare minimum profits to the host countries while maximizing profits for the parent companies. Straight tax evasion, such as is practiced by the relatively primitive local enterprise, does not seem to be necessary in the case of foreign companies. Instead, experts dispatched by the parent company can take maximum advantage of all possible legal loopholes, of which there are many in the imperfect laws of Latin America.

There is circumstantial evidence that tax avoidance of this sort happens in Latin America on a large scale. Nor does the extent of these practices depend only upon the size of differentials in the tax levels between the host country and the home country of the parent, as some students of corporate behavior assume. Purely economic considerations explain only partly the behavior of international companies. The decision to minimize profits abroad and maximize those of the parent company may also be related to the need for surplus funds for investment in other foreign countries. Or else the practice may respond to the difference in values that are attached to a high

level of profits in different societies. If high
profits are declared by a subsidiary in a Latin American country, that fact might stir up political opposition and the envy of competitors; but outstanding
financial performance reported by a parent company
located in a developed nation will be taken as proof
of the acumen of its management and will add to the
prestige of the firm.

Those who take the position that the profits of
foreign controlled enterprises are actually similar
to those in their home countries (and thus lower
than profits of local industrialists) will have to
explain why foreign companies are so secretive about
their overseas financial results. They do not even
show any enthusiasm for disclosing the detailed results of overseas operations to their own sharehold-
ers at home, as was pointed out in a survey made by
the National Industrial Conference Board in early
1965. According to this study:

> . . . more than 80 per cent of manufactur-
> ers surveyed earn money through exports,
> foreign licensing agreements or overseas
> manufacturing. About half have increased
> earnings from such sources in recent years.
> Yet few share the good news with their stock-
> holders. Any reader of annual reports will
> find that vital information on foreign sales
> and earnings generally is lacking, buried in
> small print in footnotes or discussed in
> terms a layman cannot understand.[15]

Suspicions in Latin American minds regarding the
real profitability of foreign-controlled corporations
are further strengthened by the present public debate
in the United States and the United Kingdom concerning the impact of foreign investment on the respective balance of payments of these countries. Corporations of those countries with branches and subsidiaries abroad have been submitting voluminous
evidence to the effect that the homeward flow of
profits and royalties and the earnings from exports
generated by their overseas subsidiaries exceed the
outflow of private capital in the long run. Although

these arguments are being expressed by large international corporations for home consumption, Latin
Americans regard them as further evidence that overseas operations are considerably more profitable
than is generally admitted. Indeed, many Marxist and
non-Marxist economists alike accept the view that
the unrestricted flow of foreign private investment
into any developing region represents in a long-run
a real cost to the economy, which rarely can be compensated by the transfer of technology, the expansion of productive capacity, or the general modernizing effect of foreign entrepreneurship coming from
the advanced countries.[16] The secretiveness of
foreign-owned corporations in the host countries is
taken as supporting evidence for this thesis. It is
said to explain also why in so many cases the highest executive posts are denied to the nationals of a
host country, unless people can be found offering
useful links to the economic policy makers of the
host country or can be considered "true" company men.

The situation of the foreign-owned corporation
presents a difficult dilemma both for the corporation
and for the host country. If the corporation repa-
triates most of its profits, as is usually the case
in activities based on natural resources, the company
is accused of draining the country of scarce foreign
exchange. If the company follows a policy of profit
reinvestment as so often happens in manufacturing,
it risks the accusation of trying to increase its
control over the national economy and of aggravating
in the long-run the host country's balance-of-payments position. Meanwhile, the developing countries
themselves are unsure whether to foster a policy of
early repatriation of profits by foreign-controlled
enterprises or to promote their reinvestment in the
domestic economy.

In principle, the growth of foreign indebtedness need not be of particular concern in an expanding economy, providing that the net income out of
which the indebtedness can be serviced grows correspondingly. But a situation may occur, as demon-
strated in such widely separated places as Australia,
Canada, and Mexico, in which the rapid growth of the

foreign-controlled sector of the economy is possible
simply by the reinvestment of profits and without an
additional inflow of external capital and new technology. When foreign-owned corporations decide for
reasons of their own to start repatriating their
profits, the balance-of-payments problem which that
decision generates can be overwhelming, requiring
all sorts of painful internal adjustments for the
national economy. The question then arises whether
the reinvestment of profits over an extended period
of time is worth the eventual cost to the host country.

    This issue is very much in the minds of economic-
policy makers not only in Latin America but in other
capital receiving countries as well. One student of
the Australian experience put it in the following way:

        . . . one suspects that for some countries
        there may be a basic incompatibility be-
        tween the economic objectives of fostering
        very rapid industrial development and at
        the same time promoting domestic full em-
        ployment at all times regardless of the
        state of foreign balance, and the accept-
        ance of an unlimited, unknown and uncon-
        trollable foreign liability.[17]

    In Latin America, where the goals of rapid in-
dustrialization and increased employment have the
highest priority, formulas are being sought to reconcile these objectives with the risks involved in
foreign claims controlled by large international
corporations. Raul Prebisch obviously had this problem in mind when he said:

        . . . a partnership between foreign and
        Latin American enterprise might be a
        very suitable solution, from the stand-
        point both of dissemination of techniques
        and of improved relations with domestic
        interests. . . . Otherwise, foreign in-
        vestment might carry undue weight in some
        branches of economic activity, which would
        be undesirable from various points of
        view.[18]

Another leading Latin American economist, refer-
ring concretely to the case of Mexico, presented the
issue with still greater frankness:

> Mexico can afford to continue absorb-
> ing foreign private capital only if it
> lets domestic capital participate in ex-
> isting foreign enterprises. Otherwise,
> the growth of profits and their transfer
> abroad will create a heavy burden upon
> the country's balance of payments.[19]

The problem would probably present itself in a
much less acute form were it not for the high and
growing cost of the transfer of modern technology to
the developing countries. Much of the advanced industrial technology developed in capitalist countries is generated by large corporations under the
auspices of the state and with its financial support.[20] The control of this technology by large
corporations is used as one of the main arguments
why the development process in Latin America and
other underdeveloped areas must be left largely in
private enterprise hands. Latin Americans suspect,
however, that they are being charged an excessive
price for the technology. The resulting financial
drain is even more difficult to deal with when the
patent licenses or the technology are considered as
a part of the capital contribution, on which profits are expected to be made over a long span of
time.[21] The alternative for the developing countries with balance of payments difficulties would be
to use outmoded second-class technology, which may
be obtained practically free. But such a policy, it
is said in the area, would amount to the perpetua-
tion of backwardness and "technological colonialism."

Of late, Latin Americans have placed increased
priority emphasis on the need for massive transfers
of technology and on the divorcement of those transfers from the inflow of private capital. Commercial
arrangements covering the transfer of foreign industrial technology under "reasonable" terms are to be
preferred to direct investment because such arrangements have the merit of keeping control of important

sectors of the economy in the hands of nationals;
hence, it is felt, they do not constitute a direct
competitive threat to domestically-owned and techni-
cally weak enterprises.[22] When licensing arrangements are made between a foreign parent and its subsidiary, the arrangements are viewed with strong
suspicion as they are considered a means to evade
taxes on profits; what is in fact profit is labeled
as a licensing charge or technical assistance fee
and becomes a cost of doing business for tax purposes in the host country. Some Latin Americans
also insist that inter-company licensing amounts
simply to a division of markets for the benefit of
the international parent, a parcelling out of exclusive rights to sell. Similar opinions in Australia,
Brazil, Canada and Mexico suggest that there may be
some substance in these assumptions.

Finally, the insistence on the part of international corporations that ownership and control of
the foreign subsidiary must rest in the hands of
their own nationals represents an additional source
of conflict. The strong feelings in the host countries on subjects of this sort again have their origin in a mixture of economic and socio-political considerations. The importation of foreign management
personnel and the rejection of local capital participation confirm to Latin American minds that foreign-
owned companies do not want to become an integral
part of the local societies.[23] These personnel policies also are said to represent a major obstacle to
the spreading of managerial know-how in the capital-
receiving country and to the growth of the domestic
entrepreneurial class.

Research undertaken in Brazil and Mexico demon-
strates that these practices are contrary to the
best interests of the foreign-controlled enterprises
themselves.[24] Foreign companies using nationals for
their managerial positions in these two countries
were found to be doing much better than the firms
that had been fully manned from abroad. This was
the case partly because executives sent from the
parent country were not more efficient than locally
drafted management personnel; at the same time, they

were much more expensive, much less adaptable to local conditions, and much less capable of training
others for eventual positions as managers in the enterprise. Many of these executives were obsessed
with the need for job protection, and were unwilling
to acknowledge the possibility that local personnel
could qualify to take over.[25]

The unwillingness of foreign firms to share ownership of their local subsidiaries with nationals by
selling equity in the incipient Latin American capital markets represents another source of friction.
Local entrepreneurs and financial intermediaries see
themselves robbed of an opportunity to participate
in highly profitable activities. The fact that foreign companies frequently resort to the local banking systems for short and medium credit adds to the
bitterness. In inflationary economies, the competition for banking credit is very severe. For a number of reasons, large foreign-controlled corporations
have relatively easy access to these credit sources.
Accordingly, a local entrepreneur sees himself at a
double disadvantage. He cannot buy his way into
many dynamic foreign controlled enterprises; but at
the same time his possibilities of getting banking
credit are curtailed by the borrowing activities of
these same foreign-controlled enterprises.

There are many reasons why international corporations are often unwilling to share their management
and ownership prerogatives with local interests.
Some of these reasons are vaguely philosophical.
But some are quite explicit and are described with
disarming frankness by publications directed to corporate executives. The most powerful argument
against joint capital ventures overseas is the restraint which they impose on an international corporation's effort to maximize its worldwide sales and
profits. With rapidly changing market conditions,
successful companies are expected to be able frequently to adjust strategy and tactics: to be in
position, for example, to shut down redundant plants,
to alter the product mix in a given plant, to integrate the production of one plant with that of others
in different national markets, to shift the sourcing

for some market from one plant to another, and s
As the markets of the world are rapidly integrat
and as national barriers disappear because of economic integration schemes, firms may often find their
subsidiaries competing with each other. The corporation with full control of its foreign affiliates will
have no trouble reallocating the markets in terms of
production and sales. But when outside capital par-
ticipates in each different local venture, there are
infinite possibilities of potential conflict.

> Dissension often arises over the dis-
> position of profits--whether to distribute
> or reinvest, whether to expand and when to
> do so. Such basic decisions as what to
> manufacture and how to sell are bones of
> contention. There are built-in clashes
> over the determination of royalties, inter-
> corporate fees, and, most important, prices.
> Questions of general management philosophy,
> ranging from financial and accounting prac-
> tices and accuracy of tax returns to com-
> pensation and control of personnel, contin-
> ually frazzle executive nerves.[26]

To sum up, the sources of conflict and friction
between large international corporations and the
transitional societies of Latin America are numerous
and varied. First, one sees a clash of philosophies--
an insistence on the unlimited benefits of free enterprise and private capital on the one hand, confront-
ing a profound suspicion of capitalism and foreign
private investment on the other. Then, there is the
insistence of foreign business on its right to secretiveness regarding its operations, posed against
the deep-rooted concern of the tension-ridden transitional societies that the presence of foreign capital robs it of large part of the fruits of development. If this were not enough, one sees how the insistence by large corporations on a "favorable investment climate" runs head-on into the conviction
of the developing societies that a meaningful independent and political existence implies some measure
of control over domestic resources and economic policies. All this is further complicated by the resis-

tance to large corporations' efforts to link the
transfer of modern technology with the inflow of private foreign capital, as against the receiving country's desire for foreign technology without foreign
control. Additional conflicts arise because capital
exporters insist upon imposing their own management
personnel and maintaining full financial control of
foreign operations while the capital importing countries try for the nationalizing of management and
for domestic capital participation in activities considered vital for economic development. These conflicts resemble in many respects those that are found
in Australia or Canada. If they are much more acute
in Latin America, it is because that region is still
much behind in economic and political development.

REGIONAL DEVELOPMENT AND FOREIGN INVESTMENT

The doctrine of Latin American regional economic
development was first fostered by the Economic Commission for Latin America in the early 1950's, at a
time when the southern part of the Western Hemisphere
was about to be plunged into a period of serious economic difficulties. The period from the outbreak of
World War II to the end of the Korean hostilities
had been years of relatively rapid advance for the
area. Between 1940 and 1955, three major Latin American republics (Argentina, Brazil and Mexico) and
some of the lesser ones (Chile, Colombia and Peru)
registered impressive progress in diversifying their
exports and industrializing their economies.

During this period of growth, foreign private
capital continued to play an important role in the
export-oriented sector, but the industrialization
process was mainly fostered by domestic savings and
domestic entrepreneurs. At that time, Latin American markets were too small to attract large industrial enterprises from advanced countries. In the early
1950's, however, local import replacement policies
started to gather strength; at that stage, foreign
industrial corporations decided to move into Latin
America in order to hurdle the increasing import
barriers and to take advantage of the mounting protection against import competition.

The promoters of the new Latin American economic development ideology, therefore, launched their ideas at a time when foreign manufacturing investment in the region was still insignificant. Despite this fact, ECLA ideology from the first expressed a clear preference for public capital over private. This preference was based on two considerations: first, highest priority was given to the expansion of social overhead facilities, and such facilities could only be financed from public sources; second, private capital was simply too expensive, in light of the difficult balance-of-payment situation of the region.[27]

In the latter 1950's, as the Latin American Free Trade Area and the Central American Common Market projects began to take shape, there was little time to reassess the role of foreign private investment. By then, national industrialization programs were running into serious difficulties because of the limited size of effective domestic markets and the misallocation of available resources. Leaders of the Latin American economic integration programs were fully occupied trying to understand the causes of these difficulties. The diagnosis which emerged took the following lines:

Between 1940 and 1955, Latin American development had been following the pattern of nineteenth century Europe and the United States, concentrating mainly on consumer goods industries; these could be established with relatively modest investment outlays and inexpensive technology. But by the midfifties, the major republics of Latin America had almost completed this stage of industrialization; the climate was now ready for entry into the second stage: building up a heavy industrial base. The development of new heavy industrial activities, however, was hampered by a number of factors. The most important perhaps was that by the mid-fifties the capacity of Latin American countries to finance increased imports had stopped expanding, with the exception of Mexico, Peru, and Venezuela. Moreover, the establishment of heavy industrial activities implied access to modern technology and large-scale operations, unless the level of protection against

imports was to be raised beyond reason. Furthermore,
governmental policies had not yet been introduced
which would increase mass purchasing power sufficiently to absorb large-scale output, and would improve
educational systems sufficiently to generate the
necessary skilled industrial labor force. In short,
despite public pressures for continued and acceler-
ated industrialization, Latin America still lacked
many of the prerequisites. Although an impressive
natural resources base was present, the social overhead facilities, capital resources, human skills,
access to technology and size of domestic markets
were hardly commensurate with the establishment of
heavy industries.

To break the impasse, the new regional development proposals placed their main emphasis on increased
regional trade. The two integration programs, launched
in 1960, left for future action the difficult problems
of internal reforms in the member countries and adjustment in trade and aid policies on the part of the
advanced countries, though solutions to these problems
were obviously necessary for the acceleration of Latin
America's growth. Despite their incomplete character,
these ECLA-sponsored proposals had strong political
and even emotional appeal for the growing Latin American intellectual and technical elites, for they suggested a way of ending the domination of the region
by impersonal outside forces and a way of arresting
the progressive disintegration of the area through
the stifling effect of increased obstacles to the
intra-regional movement of goods, services, and
people.

The Montevideo Treaty, which established the
framework for the Latin American Free Trade Area, was
considered by its authors and the participating countries as only the first step on a long and difficult
road toward regional economic cooperation. In spite
of the patent weaknesses in the major clauses of the
Treaty, its preamble clearly links trade liberalization with cooperation and coordination in other
fields of crucial importance to the acceleration of
the development process in the area. The Treaty
sets as a final goal the gradual emergence of a

Latin American Common Market. Some leaders in the
region, following in the footsteps of the Latin American ideologists of the early nineteenth century,
even see in the far distant future the emergence of
political union.

    With regard to a possible role for foreign capi-
tal in the region's development, the Montevideo
Treaty is characteristically laconic. The relevant
provision, which appears in Article 15, merely com-
mits the Contracting Parties to reconcile "the treatment they accord to capital, goods and services from
outside the Area." In addition, import and export
regimes are to be reconciled "in order to assure
fair competitive conditions . . . and to facilitate
the increasing integration and complementarity of
their economies." In mentioning foreign capital,
the Treaty drafters were obviously concerned that
members of the free trade area might begin competing
for foreign private investment, for the purpose of
getting the upper hand in the region's industrialization. They were also concerned that the more backward republics might not be able to attract any foreign private capital at all for industrial development. Thus, foreign capital and modern technology
might have been attracted to the industrial development poles already existing in Argentina, Brazil,
and Mexico, especially if these countries were left
free to offer new incentives to prospective investors.
Consequently, the distances in the development levels
within the region would grow instead of diminishing.

    It is worth noting that the Treaty of Montevideo
simply expressed the need for a reconciliation of
treatment afforded to foreign capital but did not
attempt to define what kind of reconciliation was advisable. Should the treatment of foreign capital be
equal in all member countries? Should an agreement
take the form of a regional code for foreign investment? Should it cover all forms of foreign investment or simply foreign direct investment in new manufacturing activities? Nowhere in the Treaty or the
annexed protocols can answers to these questions be
found. By common consent, it was decided that these
matters should be considered in light of the LAFTA
experiences.

A survey of foreign investment in Latin America
was launched under the joint auspices of ECLA and
the Organization of American States (OAS) shortly after the signing of the Montevideo Treaty.[28] The
issue proved to be very much in the minds of Latin
American government and business circles. Preoccupation centered around one of the problems mentioned
earlier: the possibility that governments might com-
pete to attract foreign investment into sectors expected to produce industrial goods for the whole free
trade area, and the related possibility that such
foreign-controlled enterprises might drive local establishments out of business. Noting these fears,
the ECLA-OAS study recommended further regional in-
quiries into the feasibility of establishing a common policy toward foreign private capital.

The Managua Treaty, creating a Central American
Common Market, did not take any position on the subject of regional policies toward foreign private capital. Nevertheless, apprehensions about the undue
influence of foreign enterprises emerged shortly after the establishment of the Common Market. These
apprehensions found their reflection in clauses in-
corporated in two agreements signed in 1963 by the
five member countries, on the occasion of the establishment of the first so-called integration industries; the occasion for these agreements was the
authorization of certain specific industrial projects, which would enjoy immediate access to all
parts of the regional market and which would be protected during a ten-year period from the possibility
that additional plants might be set up in the area.
Both agreements provide explicitly for the participation of Central American capital in the favored projects. In the case of a soda ash and insecticides
plant to be established in Nicaragua, a minimum of
40% Central American capital was agreed upon; in
that of a tire plant in Guatemala, local interests
are to have a majority participation.[29]

With the increasing flow of foreign private capital into the area, following the establishment of
the Central American Common Market, local preoccupation with economic and political implications of

this phenomenon clearly gathers strength. In the
summer of 1965 ministers of economy of five Central
American republics found it advisable to sign a
joint declaration to the effect that although the
scarcity of domestic savings makes it necessary to
complement such savings with foreign capital, nevertheless local capital resources and native entrepreneurship should play the fundamental role in the
region's economic development. Consequently, the
declaration goes on, both the governments of the member countries and regional agencies should foster
the establishment of joint industrial ventures whenever the size of new industrial projects and the
lack of access to modern technology make it difficult to mobilize regional financial resources and
entrepreneurial skill, but in the remaining cases
clear priority should be given to projects controlled
by the region's nationals. Furthermore, in the case
of new projects initiated by foreign corporations,
Central American investors should receive an option
to buy into these enterprises with the financial
help, if necessary, of Central American regional and
national development institutions.[30]

The LAFTA experiences during its first five
years of existence do not throw too much light on
the subject of future relations between the Latin
American integration program and foreign private capital. In the first three years following the signature of the Montevideo Treaty, net foreign investment
in Latin American manufacturing activities continued
to grow, reaching a total of $220 million for all
19 republics in 1962. In the early fifties, the comparable figure had been $125 million annually. There
was a steep drop in foreign manufacturing investment
in Brazil, due to the domestic political situation
after 1960, and there was considerable increase of
foreign investment in consumer goods and petroleum
refining in the Central American Common Market. In
general, however, foreign private capital investment
in Latin America in the early years of the 1960's
followed the patterns of the previous decade, responding to market opportunities offered mainly by
the more developed countries in the area. In spite
of exhortations of many business journals in the in-

dustrial countries and in spite of accusations by
the Latin American extreme left to the effect that
the regional integration programs represented a new
form of "foreign imperialist domination," the large
international corporations continued to react in the
traditional way, adjusting their production policies
and investment decisions to the particular conditions
of particular markets.

Thus far, therefore, foreign investors have
shown little interest in exploiting the opportunities offered by the Latin American regional integration projects. This may be due to the fact that the
first four annual tariff negotiations conducted in
LAFTA have concentrated on traditional intra-zonal
commodity trade, rather than on new possibilities.
It may also be due to the fact that many Latin American entrepreneurs have resisted lowering tariffs on
industrial goods, and that state-owned or state-con-
trolled heavy industries have shown an equal lack of
enthusiasm for regional cooperation. Corporations
with long experience in Latin America have in any
case been conditioned by the autarchic industrialization policies followed in the area in the postwar
period. No evidence is yet available, therefore,
that foreign industrial enterprises operating in
Latin America attach great importance to benefits
arising from the large-scale operations and economies
of scale which may yet emerge from these regional
projects.[31] As long as adequate market protection,
country by country, is available, subsidiaries of
foreign corporations are ready to accept the restraints imposed by the size of the market in spite
of unused capacity and multiplication of plants.

What seems to be important for a big international corporation is not only profits but its
presence in any large developing country with long-
run growth possibilities. Its presence in such countries permits the enterprise "to keep a foot in the
door," permitting a rapid adjustment to new situations such as the emergence of a regional market.
Large international corporations, therefore, are
neither leaders nor promoters of regional integration programs. They are willing to accept autarchic

policies as long as control over their operations is
not challenged. If and when a regional economic integration program is set in motion, they may or may
not take advantage of such developments; they may
foster or hinder it, according to their global interests and the strategy of each constituent corporation in the system.

The cautious policy so far displayed by international corporations operating in LAFTA countries
has not dispelled the misgivings of Latin Americans.
In 1963, when LAFTA was in the third year of its existence, two members of the Panel of OAS Experts on
the Alliance for Progress observed that Latin America
still feared the dominance of foreign enterprises in
a common market arrangement.[32]

They echoed a statement made earlier the same
year by Raul Prebisch who said:

> There is a general concern [in the
> area] lest foreign enterprise . . . make
> better use of the vast opportunities for
> trade that are emerging in the member
> countries and assume a leading role in
> complementarity agreements and in the area
> in general. Unless the risk is averted,
> this great undertaking will not be able to
> advance very far because of the formidable
> opposition it is liable to provoke.[33]

At the Third Annual Conference of LAFTA in 1963,
the Secretariat was instructed to collect from member
governments all available information on foreign
direct investment and to transmit the information to
the LAFTA Advisory Commission on Monetary Affairs.
The initiative was stimulated by the fact that negotiations were soon to be undertaken on a common list
of commodities to be granted free trade rights inside the area. According to the provisions of the
Montevideo Treaty, a schedule of such commodities
was to be negotiated at three-year intervals, and
the first schedule was to cover 25% of the value of
the intra-zonal trade. Unlike the tariffs which had
been reduced as a result of the annual negotiations

provided for in the Treaty, tariffs for commodities
put on the so-called common list were not subject to
any further negotiations and could not be reestab-
lished by renegotiation.

In the spring of 1964, the LAFTA Advisory Commission on Monetary Affairs found that a coordination
of policies toward foreign private investment would
be highly advisable, but that the task was far from
easy because of the conflicting interests and policies of the member countries. The Commission noted
that the individual countries of LAFTA apply to a
diverse array of foreign investment policies, ranging
from the most liberal treatment to the most restrictive measures. Consequently, any possible coordin-
ated action would have to be taken by stages.[34]

In the opinion of the LAFTA Commission, all member countries first would have to agree to "freeze"
their foreign investment legislation or at least to
refrain from introducing new incentives exceeding
those existing in the countries with the most liberal provisions. Later, countries would have to
apply "common treatment" in three concrete fields:
(a) capital movements, and transfers of profits, interest, royalties and technical assistance fees;
(b) imports of machinery and equipment not produced
in the zone, for new industrial plants and the modern-
ization of antiquated industrial facilities; (c) re-
valuation of assets of foreign-owned enterprises for
fiscal purposes. In the final stage, there would
have to be regional consideration and reconciliation
of fiscal and exchange incentives such as acceler-
ated depreciation schemes and tax freezes for foreign
enterprises, and bilateral or multilateral agreements
covering double taxation and convertibility. No progress seemed possible in the short run, however, on
efforts to harmonize national policy measures covering restrictions on the entry or participation of
foreign capital in individual countries.

The Commission also recommended setting up a
permanent consultative organ within LAFTA which
would act as a watchdog over foreign investment policies of individual countries and would attempt to

harmonize them progressively. Such an organ also
would do the spadework for joint future action in
the world capital markets, aimed at mobilizing external resources for specific large industrial investment projects meant to serve the whole region and,
particularly, for enterprises to be located in the
less developed member countries. The same LAFTA
body would be in charge of promoting the association
of private capital originating in the area itself in
order to generate enterprises producing for the whole
zone. Such joint Latin American ventures, in fact,
have been emerging slowly in the past few years, as
Argentine and Mexican capital has bought into small
and medium-sized enterprises in the least developed
countries of the area.

Along with these preliminary probings into problems involving the reconciliation of different foreign investment regimes within LAFTA, pressures have
been building up for the strengthening of regional
financial institutions; the function of such institutions would be to provide credit and technical assistance to the Latin American private sector, thus re-
dressing somewhat the balance between local private
enterprise and foreign-owned corporations. The Inter-
American Development Bank, established shortly before
the signature of the Montevideo and Managua treaties,
has been making continuous efforts to become the
"economic integration bank." It gives high priority
(though without much tangible results, so far, one
must confess) to public or private projects of multi-
national scope in this region; it has established a
special fund for financing intra-zonal trade in capital goods; and it is actively fostering economic development programs in the border zones of neighbor-
ing LAFTA members, both present or prospective. In
Central America, the sub-regional development bank,
Banco Centroamericano de Integración Económica, has
been attempting with some success to accomplish similar tasks.

In the case of LAFTA, however, all these efforts
are considered as falling short of the region's needs.
In view of the general dissatisfaction with LAFTA's
role in accelerating the economic development in

Latin America, a movement was started in 1963 aimed
at broadening the integration process. Concrete proposals were made in late 1964 and early 1965, not
only by four experts on LAFTA (Raul Prebisch, José
Antonio Mayobre, Felipe Herrera and Carlos Sanz de
Santamaría) but also independently by a group of experts from the Inter-American Development Bank.
There was agreement that the Montevideo Treaty had
led to a considerable increase of intra-zonal trade--
from $350 million annually at the beginning of the
decade to nearly $600 million in 1964. In spite of
a sizable trade expansion, however, the bulk of the
commodity flows within the LAFTA still consisted of
foodstuffs and other primary commodities. Tariff
concessions extended multilaterally in the first
four annual rounds of LAFTA negotiations had had
little effect on the composition and direction of
trade among the member countries, except in the case
of the two most dynamic Latin American economies,
Mexico and Peru. At least until the end of 1963,
manufactures represented a negligible element in
LAFTA's total commercial exchange.

Besides, no coordination of economic development policies had been achieved, in spite of efforts
within LAFTA, the OAS, and the Alliance for Progress.
Industrial cooperation had been limited in practical
terms to a few industrial "complementarity agreements" of marginal importance; and even these had required the initiative of foreign-controlled enterprises. Regional transport and communication policies were still in the study stage. And after a
score of regional meetings, all attempts in the
field of monetary and financial cooperation had re-
sulted merely in an uncoordinated list of proposals
and in the establishment of the LAFTA Financial and
Monetary Council which is expected to serve as a
meeting place for consultations among central banks
in the area.

Some of the reasons for the disappointing progress in trade liberalization within the region are
obvious. Unlike the European Economic Community and
the European Free Trade Area, there are no provisions
in LAFTA for automatic across-the-board tariff reduc-

tions, aimed at the removal of substantially all restrictions on existing or potential trade among member countries. Tariff reductions are negotiated
product-by-product; quantitative targets and specific
time limits for the reduction and elimination of restrictions are of little practical effect; and member
countries retain the right to withdraw negotiated
tariff concessions as long as they are not included
in the common schedule. Behind the weakness of the
trade liberalization mechanisms lie various pressures.
In the large countries, these pressures originate to
a considerable extent from fear of the competition
which might sweep an enlarged free trade zone. In
the smaller countries the pressures stem from a mere
general feeling of helplessness. The fears grow
more acute when the possible entry of large international corporations into the LAFTA market is envisaged.
As we observed earlier, these industrial giants are
thought to be well equipped to supply the whole of
Latin America from a few plants strategically located
in the major countries.

Thus far, as we noted, the investment decisions
of foreign capital in Latin America have hardly been
affected by LAFTA's emergence. But there is indirect
evidence that the situation could change rapidly if
LAFTA were to accelerate its trade liberalization programs. LAFTA's developments are followed in detail
by the international financial press and by specialized publications destined for corporate executives
in the United States and Western Europe. The general
tenor of the comments in these publications is that
LAFTA may become a going concern in the not-too-
distant future and that businessmen should prepare
their strategy for the eventuality. In some foreign
business circles, however, an even more ambitious
and rather different theme has emerged. High executives of large mining, banking, and public utilities
corporations with widespread interests in Latin
America have been publicly extolling the virtues of
regional integration programs; but their conception
of such programs would comprehend the whole of the
Western Hemisphere, including the United States and
Canada. These declarations have been coupled with
the view that the United States business community

"can take the leadership in promoting the Latin American common market," provided that United States official agencies abandon their government-to-government aid policies; these policies, it is contended,
create "a different attitude on the part of some governments toward the private sector" and worsen "the
environment of private capital development in Latin
America."[35]

In the eyes of Latin American nationalist
elites, both from the left and the right, such statements represent new evidence that the interest of
foreign corporate executives in LAFTA and the Central American Common Market originates in purely
pecuniary considerations. Such statements are
thought to demonstrate the unwillingness of foreign
capital to come to terms with Latin America's political and economic objectives, which require that foreign capital should play only a secondary role. To
the extreme radicals, the insistence of large for-
eigh corporations on full participation in the
fruits of regional economic cooperation proves that,
after all, the economic integration of Latin America
is part and parcel of a "grand design" to control
the region's destiny from outside. At the same time,
local entrepreneurs, especially small and medium industrialists, harden their anti-integration attitudes, bolstered in their conviction that a common
market's industrial activities will be taken over by
a few large foreign corporations.

All this helps to explain why the most recent
proposals for strengthening LAFTA place stress not
only on the overhaul of the trade liberalization
mechanisms but also on the coordination of regional
investment policies. A certain degree of coordination
in the two fields seems imperative also in view of the
fear among the poorest members of the group that they
may suffer from the regional trade arrangements. The
problem of unequal distribution of gains from economic integration, as we indicated earlier, has
haunted LAFTA from its very beginnings.

Accordingly, more and more thought is being
given in Latin America to the establishment of some

sort of regional compensation mechanism which would give special support to the least developed of the member countries. The idea is gaining ground that an effective coordination of regional investment policy might be the means of ensuring a more equal distribution of gains in the future Latin American common market. Such a policy would "concentrate on the countries that are relatively less developed and on any country in which the process of integration might give rise to substantial difficulties."[36]

In the opinion of an ECLA technical study, any successful regional investment policy would involve a prior agreement in the area about the role of the foreign capital in Latin America's future economic development. The study concludes:

> The crux of a healthy Latin American nationalism lies not only in the vigorous promotion of the region's development and the improvement in living standards of its people but also in the stimulation of regional capital, permitting it to play a decisive role, and the establishment of conditions for self-sustained and independent development.
> The regional investment policy should assure that foreign capital is absorbed under conditions compatible with the region's external indebtedness capacity and the independence of the development process.[37]

Latin American economic ideology, it is clear, has come a very long way in ten years. During the 1954 OAS meeting of ministers concerned with economic issues, proposals submitted for the liberalization of Latin American trade were nothing more than technical suggestions, without political or ideological content. Ten years later, economic integration programs were being envisaged as an expression of "a healthy Latin American nationalism" and "the independence of the development process." Unfortunately, these deep changes are little understood in the outside world. And this lack of understanding only magnifies the

frictions between Latin American societies and foreign private capital.

The establishment of a modus vivendi between
Latin American societies and foreign private capital
would involve a series of profound adjustments on
various levels. First and foremost, such a modus
vivendi would require a complete overhaul of the
political policies of the United States towards the
region, since these are largely determined by the
attitudes towards Latin American problems which are
prevalent in international corporations. For a
short time after the establishment of the Alliance
for Progress in 1961 it was widely hoped that this
new hemispheric mechanism would help to alleviate
tensions in the area and to accelerate economic development by rallying Latin America's modernizing
forces around the ideas of economic regional cooperation. But the mechanisms of the Alliance for Progress broke down at a very early stage. By mid-1965,
practically no one in Latin America and very few
people elsewhere believed that it could be infused
with new life.[38]

The Alliance for Progress had little chance of
success from its very beginning, because of its internal contradictions in aims. Whatever chances it
had, however, were destroyed by later developments.
The plain fact is that the effective economic growth
of Latin America must inevitably be accompanied by
increasing political independence.[39] Yet, this is a
fact which the United States is not prepared to acknowledge or accept.

Accordingly, the charter creating the Alliance
for Progress attempts to suppress the basic dilemma.
Regional economic integration, though dealt with in
detail, is only remotely related to the economic development of the area as a whole. And measures are
promoted and financed on the basis of a series of
bilateral bargains with the United States, the only
exception being the activities of the Inter-American
Development Bank. As a result, the client position
of most Latin American republics vis-à-vis United
States is underlined and the forces in each country

which consider regional integration and cooperation
schemes as inimical to their "special" relationship
with the aid-dispensing country are strengthened. In
the light of United States willingness to extend bilateral rewards for good behavior, those who defend
regional economic integration programs in Latin America are under constant pressure from Latin American
practitioners of Realpolitik to justify any emphasis
on the well-being of the region as a whole.

Whatever complex reasons are behind its failure,
the Alliance for Progress has never become a truly
multilateral mechanism. On the United States side,
the position has been that Congress would under no
circumstances relinquish its control of the use of
United States aid funds, except those specifically
voted for international institutions. At the same
time, most Latin American governments have preferred
a bilateral bargaining process rather than a multilateral distribution of aid. The revision of United
States policy towards economic integration in Latin
America, therefore, would involve a number of steps
which seem unlikely in the present climate of inter-
American relations. They would have to include:
(1) establishing a Latin American OEEC, and divorcing
economic aid programs from its present bilateral approach; (2) organizing Latin American economic aid
programs on a long-range basis for the purpose of
achieving growth, and not disbursing aid for the purpose of buying diplomatic allies and satisfying domestic interest groups; (3) mobilizing additional
aid for Latin America from Western Europe, a task
obviously impossible as long as the region is considered an exclusive sphere of influence of the United States; (4) assisting Latin Americans in the
painful job of organizing and strengthening their
own regional cooperation mechanisms without remind-
ing them constantly that they are not grown up enough
to decide on appropriate policies for economic development; (5) supporting Latin American modernizing
forces in their daily battles against inhibiting
forces at home and the allies of such forces abroad;
(6) and, finally, attempting to educate United States
public opinion about the complexities of development
in transitional societies and the limited usefulness

of orthodox free-enterprise policies in the framework.

If such a program were put into action, there
would still be considerable room for cooperation between Latin American governments and private capital,
domestic or foreign.

First, however, the domestic private sectors in
the countries participating in Latin American integration programs would have to be strengthened by a
regional industrial development bank, endowed with
sizable financial resources, including outside contributions. This role could be played by an expanded
Inter-American Development Bank, although many people
in the area propose the establishment of a Latin American development corporation or a body similar in its
functions to the International Finance Corporation, a
subsidiary of the World Bank. The express function
of such an institution, whether or not linked to the
Inter-American Development Bank, would be to provide
capital resources to industrial enterprises fully-
owned or fully-controlled by Latin Americans and
oriented towards production for the region as a
whole. The regional industrial development corporation, if properly related to other integration mechanisms, could also play a decisive role in the imple-
mentation of the regional investment policy, especially in respect to the most backward member countries.

Moreover, the attitudes of foreign private capital toward Latin American nationalism would have to
change. A quarter of a century ago, on the eve of
Pearl Harbor, a United States political scientist
was already underlining the need on the part of North
Americans for a "willingness to admit Latin Americans
as partners with equal rights, and the development of
an attitude by which Latin America and its people
will not be considered primarily as objects of exploitation. . . ." As he then put it:

> This will mean, besides other things the
> gradual [italics in the text] transfer of
> ownership and management of a considerable
> part of foreign-owned enterprises to

nationals. The necessary adjustments in
this respect will have to be rather com-
prehensive. Otherwise, "el capitalismo
yanqui" will find the sociological tide
in most Latin American countries turning
against it more strongly every day.[40]

This is exactly what has happened in the intervening quarter century. Latin American nationalism
is stronger than ever, but most international corporations are frozen in the same attitudes as decades
ago. They have difficulty in understanding a point
obvious to students of the process of economic development: in transitional societies, an initial in-
clination may exist to limit the role of private
enterprise; but the moment can come when all available reserves of energy, public or private, are acceptable and when the roles of the state and private
enterprise can be complementary. As nationalist
movements become more secure in their achievements,
foreign-controlled enterprise may cease to appear ex-
clusively as a threat of foreign domination, and may
become accepted as a limited tool to accelerate
growth. This outcome depends partly on how such enterprises conduct themselves in the intervening
period of uncertainty. At the present stage of the
Latin American history, foreign private capital appears to be imperilling its opportunities for a future role by continuing its battle against large-
scale government-to-government economic aid to Latin
America and by continuing its attempts to intimidate
Latin American governments which follow nationalist
economic policies.

Meanwhile, over the more immediate period ahead,
some thinking has to be done on how such corporations
can contribute to Latin American growth on terms acceptable to Latin America. Recognizing the pressing
nature of this problem, students of international affairs have recently developed various suggestions
aimed at divorcing the transfer of technology and
capital from actual control of Latin American enterprise. Typical of some of these new proposals is
one that "United States income taxes should be for-
given on income of United States residents derived

from (1) royalty and fee payments on patent rights
conferred to foreign firms not owned by U.S. interests
[italics in the original], (2) technical and managerial assistance contracts with foreign-owned firms, and
(3) interest and dividends on portfolio investments as
distinguished from direct investment."[41]

Pressures of this sort might represent a small
step in the right direction. But many other steps
would have to be taken simultaneously, both on the
political and the economic level. To formulate and
implement such steps, a great deal of unorthodox
thinking in the advanced countries is urgently
needed.

Footnotes

1. Inter-American Economic and Social Council,
Inter-American Alliance for Progress Committee,
Needs and Availabilities of External Financial Re-
sources under the Alliance for Progress (Washington,
D.C.: June, 1964), mimeographed.

2. Victor L. Urquidi, "Some Implications of
Foreign Investment for Latin America," a lecture at
the Royal Institute for International Affairs (London: February, 1965), unpublished manuscript.

3. This desire is not limited to Latin America,
but pervades the political life of African and Asian
societies. It may be exemplified by a statement of
a leading Philippine private entrepreneur to the effect that although underdeveloped countries are eager
to attract foreign capital in some measure "their
chief fear is that of neocolonialism in the form of
a large percentage of their economies in foreign
hands." Roberto Villanueva, "New Developments in
Private Capital Transfers in the Philippines," Motivations and Methods in Development and Foreign Aid,
Society for International Development (Washington,
D.C.: 1964), p. 116.

4. Private Investment in Latin America, Report
of the Subcommittee on Inter-American Economic Relationship of the Joint Economic Committee, Congress
of the United States (Washington, D.C.: United
States Government Printing Office, 1964), p. 1.

5. Frank Brandenburg, The Development of Latin
American Private Enterprise (Washington, D.C.:
National Planning Association, 1964), pp. 19-20.

6. Claude McMillan, Jr., Richard Gonzalez with
Leo G. Erickson, International Enterprise in a Developing Economy. A Study of United States Business in
Brazil (East Lansing: Michigan State University,
1964), pp. 225-226.

7. "Informe del ex-Presidente Lleras Camargo
ante la OEA," Commercio Exterior, Mexico: February,
1963, p. 402.

8. Raul Prebisch, Towards a Dynamic Development Policy for Latin America (New York: United Nations, 1963), pp. 53-54.

9. John F. Kennedy as a Senator from Massachusetts noted in 1958 that Latin Americans "resent our
insisting upon a larger role for their private enterprise, which cannot cope with many of their problems,
or a larger role for our private investors, who have
limited their interests almost entirely to extractive industries and to only five countries (Brazil,
Cuba, Mexico, Venezuela and Chile)." The Strategy
of Peace, edited by Allen Nevins (New York: 1960),
p. 139.

10. The rejection by Latin Americans of the
IBRD-sponsored International Center for Settlement
of Investment Disputes might be better understood in
the light of a comment published in the United States:
"While the Center would have no police powers to en-
force its decisions, the inference is very plain that
a government, for instance, that failed to carry out
the terms of award could expect very little in the
way of loans from the World Bank, and quite likely
from other international or governmental lending

institutions."   Oscar E. Naumann, "World Bank Plans
New Mediation Unit for Investment Disputes," The
Journal of Commerce, New York, Nov. 6, 1964.

11. The President of the Bank of Liberia, Romeo
Horton, as quoted in an editorial "Financing the Un-
derdeveloped," The Journal of Commerce, New York,
January 22, 1963.

12. There are exceptions, however. See, for
instance, John C. Shearer, High-Level Manpower in
Overseas Subsidiaries (Princeton, N.J.:   Industrial
Relations Section, Princeton University, 1960);
McMillan, et al., op. cit., and Leland L. Johnson,
United States Private Investment in Latin America:
Some Questions of National Policy (Santa Monica,
California: Rand Corporation, July 1964).

13. Compare the same type of concern, expressed
in the Royal Commission on Canada's Economic Prospects, Final Report, November 1957 (Ottawa: Queen's
Printer and Controller of Stationery, 1958); also in
Irving Brecher and S. S. Reisman, Canada - United
States Economic Relations (Ottawa, 1957). These are
among the best analyses to date concerning the practices of foreign-controlled corporations.

14. One should note at once that official United States publications on United States foreign
direct investments contain warnings with respect to
the validity of collected data. A United States Department of Commerce study, published in 1960, notes
that "comparisons of the absolute ratios, of rates
of return, in the manufacturing industry as between
different areas abroad, or between United States and
foreign firms, are subject to so many qualifications
that all but the most general observations are likely to be invalid." United States Business Investments in Foreign Countries (Washington, D.C.:   Government Printing Office, 1960), p. 51.

15. The New York Times, April 11, 1965, "Foreign Data Held Lacking in Reports."

16. Strangely enough, in this case again, very
little serious theoretical or empirical analysis is

available. One of the few studies on the subject
concludes that there are strong indications that United States balance of payments has been favorably
affected by the operations of United States-owned
foreign enterprises in the 1950-1959 period, and
that Latin American-based enterprises were particularly helpful to the United States in this regard.
See A. Gerlof Homan, Some Measures and Interpretations of the Effects of the Operations of the United
States Foreign Enterprises on the United States Balance of Payments (Menlo Park, California: Stanford
Research Institute, August 1962).

17. Edith Penrose, "Foreign Investment and the
Growth of the Firm," The Economic Journal, London,
Vol. LXVI, No. 262, June, 1956, pp. 232, 235.

18. Prebisch, op. cit., p. 56.

19. Victor L. Urquidi's statement at a round-
table discussion on Mexico's development problems,
held in Mexico City in August 1963.

20. Over 60% of the outlay on research and de-
velopment in the United States carried out principal-
ly by large corporations and financed with government
funds. See S. C. Gilfillan, Invention and Patent
System (Materials related to continuing studies of
Technology, Economic Growth, and the Variability of
Private Investment) (Washington, D.C.: United States
Government Printing Office, 1964), p. 125.

21. A United States source estimated that United States corporations with interests abroad re-
ceived in 1963 $622 million in royalties and fees,
which represented 14% of their foreign earnings.
"Profitability of United States Foreign Investment:
What the 1963 Worldwide Record Shows," Business International, New York, Sept. 25, 1964.

22. As one witness put it in recent United
States Congressional hearings, ". . . what some of
the influential Latin Americans want is the loan of
United States foreign subsidiaries. In short, what
these ideologists want is to have their cake and eat

it, too."   Statement by Peter R. Nehemkis, Jr.,
Whirlpool Corp., in Economic Developments in South
America, hearings before the Sub-Committee on Inter-
American Economic Relationships of the Joint Economic
Committee, Congress of the United States, May 10 and
11, 1962 (Washington, D.C.:   United States Government
Printing Office, 1962), p. 52.

    23.   Similar comments of local population can
be heard about the behavior of Indian merchants in
East Africa and Lebanese businessmen in West Africa
whose practices--on the level of a small family firm--
are very similar to those of many giant foreign corporations in Latin America. No outsider is allowed
to occupy any managing position in these family firms
nor is any outside capital participation welcome.
Since similar practices are common also among older
generations of Latin American industrialists, the
corporate behavior in this respect may be not original at all, although clearly motivations of the
president of General Motors are somewhat more complicated than those of an Asian heading an export
firm in East Africa.

    24.   Shearer, op. cit., pp. 129-130, 133.

    25.   It seems, however, that lately some prog-
ress has been made in hiring national high-level manpower in Latin America. "United States Firms Overseas Going Native," Wall Street Journal, Feb. 12,
1964, and "Yanks Go Home--More United States Firms
Hire Foreigners to Manage Overseas Operations," Wall
Street Journal, March 8, 1965. The last mentioned
article quotes two interesting statements: one
attributed to Henry Ford II, chairman of Ford Motor
Co., "This is an American company and it's going to
be run from America"; another to an anonymous United
States manufacturing executive with long experience
in Latin America, "Frankly, it feels sort of funny
to see a Latin American doing your old job so well."

    26.   "Foreign Joint Ventures Raise Formidable
Barriers to Flexible Worldwide Corporate Strategy,"
Business International, New York, Sept. 4, 1964.

27. See: Economic Commission for Latin America (ECLA), International Cooperation in a Latin
American Development Policy (New York: United Nations, 1954).

28. ECLA and OAS, Foreign Private Investment
in the Latin American Free Trade Area (New York: E/CN.
12/550, 1961).

29. Protocolo al Convenio sobre el Régimen de
Industrias Centroamericanas de Integración (San Salva-
dor, January 29, 1963) reproduced in El regimen de
las inversiones privadas en el Mercado Común Centroamericano y en la Asociación Latinoamericana de
Libre Comercio (Washington: Pan American Union,
1964), pp. 207-217.

30. "Declaración de los Ministros de Economía
de Centroamérica sobre el Capital Extranjero en Centroamérica," Comercio Exterior, Mexico, July 1965,
p. 481.

31. Compare Sidney S. Dell, Latin American
Economic Integration (manuscript shortly to be pub-
lished by Oxford University Press), Chapter IX, "The
Role of Private Enterprise."

32. Harvey S. Perloff and Romulo Almeida,
"Regional Economic Integration in the Development of
Latin America," Economía Latinoamericana, (Washington:
Pan American Union, Vol. 1, No. 2, November 1963),
p. 170.

33. Prebisch, op. cit., p. 99.

34. Asociación Latinoamericana de Libre Comercio, Comision Asesora de Asuntos Monetarios, Armoni-
zación de los tratamientos aplicados a las inversiones privadas extranjeras en los países de la
Asociación Latinoamericana de Libre Comercio (ALALC/
CAM/I/di 2) Montevideo, April 20, 1964 (mimeographed).

35. A typical statement is that by Philip A.
Ray, Chairman, International Bond and Share, Inc. in
Private Investment in Latin America, Hearings before

the Subcommittee on Inter-American Economic Relationships of the Joint Economic Committee, Congress of the United States (Washington: United States Government Printing Office, 1964), pp. 22ff. Similar statements have been made by David Rockefeller, president of the Chase Manhattan Bank, by J. Peter Grace of the W. R. Grace and Co., and by George S. Moore, president of the National City Bank.

36.   See the report of Jose Antonio Mayobre, Felipe Herrera, Carlos Sanz de Santamaria, and Raul Prebisch, "Proposals for the Creation of the Latin American Common Market," reproduced in Supplement to Comercio Exterior de Mexico, Vol. XI, No. 5, May 1965, pp. 8-9.

37.   Comision Economica para America Latina (CEPAL), "Contribución a la política de integración económica de América Latina," reproduced in Hacia la integración acelerada de América Latina (Mexico: Fondo de Cultura Económica, 1965), p. 117.

38.   A recent statement by the Argentine Foreign Minister, Miguel Angel Zavala Ortiz (who by no stretch of the imagination could be considered unfriendly to the United States) illustrates this point. The New York Times, "Latin Thinks United States Perils Alliance," June 20, 1965.

39.   Merle Kling, "Towards a Theory of Power and Political Instability in Latin America," in John H. Kautsky (ed.), Political Change in Underdeveloped Countries: Nationalism and Communism (New York: John Wiley and Sons, Inc., 1962), p. 138.

40.   Richard F. Behrendt, Economic Nationalism in Latin America, Inter-American Short Papers, I, The School of Inter-American Affairs, University of New Mexico, Albuquerque, November 1941, p. 18.

41.   Johnson, op. cit., p. 72.

AN ARGENTINE VIEW

by

Enrique Garcia Vazquez

THE HISTORICAL SETTING

From the earliest days of its independence, the
Argentine Republic attracted foreign investors. In
the early 1820's, while the echoes of Argentina's
declaration of independence could still be heard,
foreigners already were exploring opportunities in
the River Plate area, in hopes of making investments
in mining, land, and agriculture.

Foreign capital did not begin to flow to Argentina in considerable volume, however, until about
1860; it was not until that time that the political
problems of integrating the country had been overcome. From that time on, however, Argentina's course
was firmly tied to the great growth of international
trade, a growth which in turn arose from the increased
industrialization of Europe, from the technological
revolution in transportation, and from the changes
in the pattern of consumer wants.

As Europe's industry grew, her demand for agricultural products from other parts of the world increased sharply. As a result, Europe looked for investment opportunities in those corners of the world
which might be potential exporters of agricultural
products. Argentina, with her great endowment of
natural resources, was an obvious target. With almost 135,000,000 acres of rich soil, especially

Enrique Garcia Vazquez is Vice President of the
Central Bank of the Republic of Argentina and a member of the faculty of the Economics Department of
the University of Buenos Aires.

adapted to agricultural and livestock production, Argentina was obviously fitted for her future role as a major agricultural exporter. Foreign investment, which up to 1860 had been insignificant, amounted in 1900 to $2.5 billions (as measured by United States dollars with the purchasing power of 1965); and, by the eve of World War I, this figure had quadrupled in amount.

In short, in the first fourteen years of the twentieth century, foreign investment in Argentina was increasing at the remarkable rate of about $550 millions per year, in terms of 1965 dollars. Most of this money was devoted to investment in the private sector, rather than to investment in public securities such as had been fashionable in the nineteenth century. Nonetheless, the effect of this investment upon the economic evolution of the country was profound, since about 75 percent of the investment was directed toward basic infrastructure such as the construction of railways.

About the time of the outbreak of World War I, some very important shifts occurred in the sources of foreign capital. Before 1900, investment from the United Kingdom had accounted for more than 80 percent of the total amount of foreign investment in Argentina. Thereafter, until the outbreak of World War I, French and German capital began to appear in considerable amounts; and by the outbreak of World War I, U.K. investments had dropped to 60 percent of the foreign total.

It was not until after World War I that U.S. capital began to appear as an important factor in the Argentine Republic. With outbreak of war, investment from Europe abruptly ceased (incidentally revealing the great external vulnerability of the economic structure of countries such as Argentina, which depend heavily upon the flow of foreign investments). The dearth of foreign capital continued through World War I and the years immediately thereafter. But beginning in 1923, one could observe a strong flow of American funds, which came to substitute for the European investments in the Argentine Republic.

American investments in the 1920's were different in a number of ways from those of the European
predecessors. In the first place, they were much
less impressive in total; American investments in
the 1920's are estimated at only about one-fifth of
the flow of European funds in the years just prior
to World War I. Accordingly, American investments
of the 1920's were much less important in the gross
fixed investment of Argentina. Whereas foreign investment in the pre-war period had represented about
45 percent of the country's gross fixed investment,
foreign investment in the 1920's accounted for bare-
ly 15 percent of the total. Fortunately, domestic
saving managed to increase at so rapid a rate between
1923 and 1930 that it completely offset the decrease
in the inflow of foreign capital and even succeeded
in doubling the aggregate flow of investment during
those seven years.

Accordingly, one may say that the first major
flow of American investment toward Argentina performed only a modest complementary role in the total
investment of the country. Its importance was less
than the earlier European investments in still another sense: By the 1920's, Argentina had already
passed through its first critical stage of economic
development. Aided by the initial flow of European
investments, the nation was already well along in
the development of infrastructure and manufacturing.
Some progressive industries were well rooted in the
country and well oriented toward modern production
techniques.

The depression which began in 1929 wholly dis-
rupted the international flow of investment. The
interruption was probably a consequence of the restrictions on international trade; but it was also
due to the decline in the savings of capital-
exporting centers, to the difficulties of the debtor
countries in meeting their liabilities, and to the
general conditions of uncertainty which affected the
world economy. The world did not manage to shake
off the effects of this crisis for many years. To
the extent that foreign private investment continued
after 1930, it tended to follow the orientation

which had characterized the U.S. investment during
the 1920's. But as the growth of the exporting sector slowed up, investments tended to shift to manufacturing which was designed to take advantage of
the broad domestic market inside Argentina. And the
import restrictions on manufactured products which
were brought about by the difficulties attending the
world payments crisis of that period stimulated this
trend even further. By 1940, American investments
in the Argentine Republic managed to reach 20 percent of total foreign investment in the country; and
in the processing and service industries, U.S. investment came to as much as 34 percent of the total.

In the years immediately following World War II,
Argentina saw the first major reversal of the long-
term growth of foreign investment in its economy.
During the war, Argentina had managed to accumulate
a considerable amount of gold and foreign currency
reserves. When the war ended, the government chose
to use about half of those reserves in order to buy
out some of the foreign investment which had existed
in the country. A widespread feeling had existed
among the people of Argentina against foreign ownership of the country's public utilities. We do not
propose to analyze the reasons for that feeling here;
it is sufficient to say that, in response to this
view, the country chose to use a major part of its
war-accumulated reserves to buy out most of the foreign interest in public services. Not all Argentine
opinion supported this purchase; on the contrary, a
very wide sector of the population considered that
the resources used to achieve the nationalization of
such enterprise might have been better used in building up the structure of the Argentine economy. Those
who hold this opinion, including the writer, believed
that the country missed a major opportunity to establish the foundations of an economic process which
would greatly have increased the country's national
product in the years that followed.

Nevertheless, the nationalization was achieved.
Thereafter, the aggregate investment in the country
dropped sharply and it took a number of years before
the capital flow picked up again. Even then, the

capital was not directed to the most appropriate sectors of the economy. Despite that fact, however, a
good part of the investment did have some dynamic effects for the nation.

WHAT ARGENTINA SEEKS FROM
FOREIGN INVESTMENT

We in Argentina have had to face real problems
with respect to certain foreign investments. I would
not be frank, nor would I be responding to the spirit
of the friendly invitation of this distinguished University, if I were to ignore those problems altogether.
On the contrary, I think it would be extremely useful
to study the reasons for these differences and to
clarify how these foreign investments are seen in the
eyes of Argentina.

First of all, it is appropriate to emphasize
that during all the long history of foreign investment in Argentina the conflicts that have arisen re-
fer to only a limited number of cases. All told,
perhaps twenty companies have been involved in such
disputes. If one bears in mind the considerable number of foreign companies that have regularly operated
in Argentina over long periods of time without en-
countering difficulties of any kind, it seems right
to say that the difficulties that have arisen have
been exaggerated out of all proportion. Such problems as have existed, it should be noted, are limited to certain specific sectors of the economy.
And these problems have not been a result of the
fact that the corporations involved were foreign-
owned; they have been due rather to the inappropri-
ateness of the conditions upon which these entities
had been permitted to operate in the first instance.

The area in which disputes with foreign enterprises have arisen is an area which the Argentine
people consider must be left to the development and
operation of the Argentine government. It would
lead us nowhere if we sought to analyze the historical process that brought about the reasons for this

fundamentally sound position. That this viewpoint
exists is an accomplished fact; and, to deal with
that fact realistically, we should define this area
precisely and we should make sure that investment
directed by the private sector is not involved in it.

The area of conflict is that of the public services and of enterprises related to the mining and
power resources of a country. As long as the direction of the economic policy of investments in that
area lies firmly in the hands of the government
through its program of direct development, the collaboration of foreign capital and technique in carrying out operations in this area raises no difficulties. Indeed, this collaboration is most important
for the efficient and rational development of the
sectors involved. Collaboration which is acceptable
takes the form of the leasing of important works and
services, executed in cooperation with the government enterprise which is in charge of policy formula-
tion in these sectors.

Cooperation between the government and the private sector has been effective for many years in
some parts of the Argentine economy. For example,
Fabricaciones Militares is an official agency which
operates a number of metalworking industries concerned with the national defense and which official-
ly promotes the development of mining resources;
through these operations, Fabricaciones Militares
establishes the guidelines for development in these
important sectors of the economy. At the same time,
there are major private enterprises in the steel
fabricating industry which perform a very adequate
complementary role, without friction or difficulty.

Another outstanding example of collaboration between the government and the private sector is represented by DINFIA, an enterprise which specializes in
the mechanical industry. DINFIA has performed well
as a training school for technical labor. Indeed,
this firm, through its training of such labor, has
been a critical force in providing the local skills
needed for a number of important enterprises in the
automotive and tractor industries in the region in
which DINFIA is located.

In a limited sector of the Argentine economy,
therefore, foreign capital is obliged to operate
within appropriate limitations. Outside of that
special area, however, there are vast sectors of
economic and productive activity in which foreign
capital can operate without any special restraint,
always provided that they conform to the very liberal laws of the country--laws whose liberal provisions I propose to comment on below.

In accordance with these terms, we in Argentina
look upon foreign investment as being highly desirable. In a world characterized by swift scientific
and technological progress, a developing country
which rejected the help of foreign capital would de-
liberately commit itself to a state of backwardness.
Technological progress is the result of enormous investment in scientific research, of a kind which is
often beyond the means of the less-developed countries and which would not be economically justified
by the still-limited markets of those countries. We
in Argentina also take the view that foreign capital
should make use of the host country's technicians and
workers and should keep open the road to the higher
management echelons of the company without discrimination based on nationality. These are views which
should be perfectly acceptable to any investor who
sees in his business activities something more than
an incidental opportunity for profit. It is a view
which contributes to development in a positive man-
ner and one which is thoroughly accepted by many
foreign companies. Indeed, many of these companies,
without being forced to do so by legislative regulations such as have been enacted in other countries,
have regularly expanded the employment of Argentine
nationals among the workers, technicians, and administrative employees of their enterprises.

We in Argentina also favor joint enterprises between foreign investors and Argentine partners; we
think of such joint ventures as being especially desirable to reduce the pressure on the balance of payments which persistently arises under the strain of
development. Joint enterprises reduce the balance-
of-payments drain which comes from the transfer of

profits. A drain of this sort, as is well known, can readily offset the inflow of capital.

The people of Argentina also favor the reinvestment of a certain proportion of the profits. We see this as a corporate contribution to the generation of domestic investment. In any case, the question of reinvestment arises only when the original investment was well conceived, so that the attraction to reinvest is particularly great. In our view, however, this kind of a decision must be taken voluntarily if it is to succeed. Any compulsory measures in this field could only lead to the ultimate failure of the policy.

Argentina does not restrict the transfer of profits by foreign companies. The only requirement for such transfers is that the payment of taxes and social contributions shall be current. In recent months, however, due to difficulties in the balance-of-payments arising out of heavy maturities of foreign debt in 1964 and 1965, the proposed remittances of foreign companies were delayed. Fortunately, the companies have fully understood the underlying reasons for this temporary situation.

As this is written, negotiations are going forward with a number of international credit agencies. As a result of these negotiations, the large profits enjoyed by such companies during 1964 and the early part of 1965 will probably soon be realized in the form of greatly increased remittances. The negotiations under consideration would integrate the refunding of Argentine foreign debt with the execution of the country's new development plan. That plan, which places heavy weight on increasing the productiveness of investments in certain sectors of agriculture and the livestock industry, foresees a major increase in Argentine exports. This increase will provide the necessary capacity for external payments which will both reinforce Argentina's foreign exchange reserves and permit the fulfillment of the country's foreign exchange commitments.

FOREIGN INVESTMENT LEGISLATION
IN ARGENTINA

The tradition of Argentina has been to grant
foreign capital the same treatment as it accords to
domestic capital.

As far back as 1818, Argentina formally agreed
to grant "national treatment" to foreigners as a
treaty right. In that year, it was embodied in the
country's commercial treaty with the United States.
That treaty provided that United States citizens
would have the right to use freely all their tangible assets in Argentina and the right to collect
profits for their use without hindrance; the only
obligation of such citizens would be to pay the same
taxes that Argentine citizens would pay in like circumstances, while enjoying all the privileges and
exemptions of Argentine nationals.

In 1853, a Treaty of Friendship, Commerce, and
Navigation was concluded with the United States.
This treaty provided categorically that citizens of
the United States would be free to enter Argentina
and to live in any part of the Argentine territory,
to deal in every type of merchandise, and to enjoy
the utmost protection and security in their business.

There is no need to recount the successive treaties that have since reaffirmed these principles.
It is worthwhile, however, to mention certain fea-
tures of the Argentine national Constitution which
serve as the basis of the Argentine legal system.
Article XX of the Constitution states that foreigners enjoy in the nation's territory all the civil
rights of citizens. They can exercise their profes-
sion, trade, or industrial activity; they can own,
buy, and sell real estate. They are also entitled
to the rights provided for the nation's residents in
the fourteenth article of the Constitution without
discrimination as between foreigners and local inhabitants; that is, they have the right, among other
things, to operate in any lawful industry and to use
and dispose of their property. As regards the use
or sale of property, the Argentine Constitution

provides that property rights are inviolable and
that any inhabitant (which certainly includes foreigners) may be deprived of his property only by a
legal determination. This means that expropriation,
which in any case is only possible when it is done
for the public benefit, must be authorized by law
and indemnification must previously have been provided.

These provisions have always been honored.
Whenever foreign capital was nationalized for any
reason, it was always done according to law and always accompanied by appropriate compensation.

The present legal regime for foreign investments was established by the Argentine Congress in
1958 in Law No. 14,780. This law once more states
the principle that foreign investment in Argentina,
whether for the promotion of new activities or for
the enlargement and improvement of those already existing, shall enjoy the same rights as those granted
to nationals. Holders of such investments may re-
patriate their profits, while the repatriation of
capital is subject only to such limitations as were
expressly agreed upon when the investment took place.

Law No. 14,780 authorizes the Executive to agree
upon the application of special measures for economic
development. On the basis of that authorization and
of the law which underlies it, the Executive in April
1964 issued Decree No. 3113. This decree aims at
promoting industrial activity in two different dimen-
sions: It provides special incentives to certain
kinds of industrial activities; and it provides
special incentives for investment in certain areas
of the country. The incentives are granted not only
to national investors but also to foreign capital,
provided that such foreign capital takes the form of
a business entity domiciled in and established by
the government of Argentina according to its laws.

The industries that are eligible for special incentives include steel, petrochemicals, cellulose,
mining, timber and forestry, fishing, hunting, and
construction. Advantages for certain specified areas

of the country are also established in order to en-
courage industrial decentralization; the advantages
are especially available for those activities which
lead to the processing of raw materials in the respective areas.

The incentives include a series of tax exemptions on facilities and profits which are available
to enterprises provided that their applications are
submitted prior to the year 1969. Preferential
prices are also provided to enterprises for gas,
electric power, fuel and transport. Capital equipment is given certain tariff and foreign exchange
advantages. And authorization is extended for the
entry of foreign personnel who are necessary to the
development of the enterprises' plans.

A final word on the legal protection to the
American investor is worth making. In 1959, the governments of the United States and Argentina concluded
an agreement which relates to a U.S. government program guaranteeing its investors against the risks of
monetary inconvertibility, that is to say, the risk
that they might be prevented from repatriating profit
or principal on investments in Argentina. According
to this agreement, the government of Argentina ack-
nowledges the right of the investor to transfer such
funds and the subrogation of the United States government with regard to them.

The legislation which I have just commented on
has one basic aim: to affirm the Argentine government's traditional support of the foreign investor
while at the same time contributing to the country's
development. The essential characteristics of that
legislation are the non-restrictive and non-discrim-
inatory treatment granted to national and foreign
capital. Although the foreign capital is given no
advantages over domestic investors, it is clear that
advantages of that sort would be neither proper nor
desirable.

THE NATIONAL DEVELOPMENT PLAN
AND FOREIGN INVESTMENT

The Argentine government has completed a national development plan, governing a five-year period from 1965 to 1969 inclusive. Many foreign experts have checked the rigorousness of the plan; indeed, the plan itself was developed with the valuable cooperation of Harvard University, a cooperation which I am pleased to acknowledge as a very effective contribution toward a better understanding of the people of the United States and Argentina. The plan has also had the benefit of the help of the private sector, through the advice of various managerial and labor groups, which were consulted during its development.

The plan analyzes the country's present situation and projects a series of national goals. To achieve those goals, it foresees an important role for financing by foreign capital. Foreign investment is expected to account for 8.5 percent of fixed gross investment during the plan period, a proportion not unlike that recorded for the last decade.

In round figures, the plan estimates that gross fixed investment for the five-year period will amount to about $16 billions. Of that total, about $1.8 billions will represent machinery and equipment from abroad. Since part of these imports will be paid out of domestic resources, the external financing should amount to about $1.4 billions. This foreign financing will come from credits granted by international agencies and by foreign suppliers of capital goods, as well as from direct investment by foreigners.

The distribution among the various sectors of the economy of the $16 billions of fixed gross investment is expected to be as follows: 17 percent to agriculture, livestock and fishing; 18 percent to industry and mining; 29 percent to power, transport and communications; 25.5 percent to housing, education, public health and water supplies; and 10.5

percent to other sectors. Of the $16 billion total,
slightly over 68 percent is to be directed to the
private sector.

Foreign financing is to have a different relative importance and a different form according to
the sector to which it contributes. In the industry
and mining area, foreign capital is to play a major
role, since its contribution will come to nearly a
quarter of the total fixed investment foreseen for
those activities. This is a sector, too, in which
the role of private entrepreneurs will be of outstanding importance. Practically all of the investment in industry and mining will come from the private sector, domestic and foreign. As far as the
foreign contribution to this sector is concerned,
somewhat more than half will arise from credits
granted by suppliers of machinery and equipment--
credits which, in turn, are often guaranteed in part
by the credit institutions of the exporting countries. Another fifth of the foreign capital will be
financed by means of credits from international agencies in order to support the acquisition of machinery and equipment on major projects. Finally, a
little more than a quarter is expected to come to
Argentina from abroad through the direct investment
route.

The plan's estimate of foreign direct investment
has been made with great care, since it represents a
sum which is somewhat less than $35 million per year.
With good luck, this figure might be increased as
the program develops; and it may be possible, accordingly, to exceed the goals set by the plan. This is
not wholly unfounded optimism; foreign investment in
the industrial sector will have to take place principally in metalworking, petrochemicals, and cellulose,
three industries in which Argentina offers great possibilities and in which import replacement for the
domestic market has still some distance to go. Accordingly, we expect our $35 million estimate to be
exceeded by a considerable margin, principally
through the appearance of new industries in these
dynamic sectors of our economy.

In the financing of the economic infrastructure, domestic saving will provide an overwhelming share of the total. Some 86.5 percent is expected to come from domestic sources, while only 13.5 percent is to come from foreign sources. Most of the foreign money for this purpose is to be channeled to the public sector.

As for the financing of housing, education, public health and water supplies, as well as the financing of agriculture, livestock and fishing, most of this will come from domestic saving. Foreign financing will be relevant only for selected imports or for some development loans not linked to imports.

Foreign financing is also of little consequence in the other sectors in which private enterprise dominates, such as trade. In these other sectors, external financing is expected to amount to only 2.7 percent of the total investment.

THE ENVIRONMENT FOR FOREIGN INVESTMENT

It has been a long time since Argentina has been in so favorable a position to carry out a program for a substantial increase in its economic growth. Unhappily, the Argentine economy has been at a complete standstill during the past fifteen years, to such an extent that the per capita gross domestic product was practically the same in 1963 as it had been in 1950. The upswing which took place in 1964, reflected in a 7 percent increase in the gross domestic product, should mark the beginning of a steady recovery; but that recovery can only be achieved by the sound execution of an adequate investment plan.

Argentina's present government took office in October 1963. One of its prime policies in the field of internal finance has been to ease the extremely tight money supply which caused such a marked decline in gross domestic product during 1962 and 1963 and which produced so much idle capacity in the country; the existence of that idle capacity was all

the more disconcerting because capacity had been increased considerably in former years through substantial imports of capital goods. Having achieved its
first objective, of reversing the down trend in production, the government has already launched on a
policy which--without imperiling the continued increase in production in the country--is intended to
achieve monetary stability as rapidly as possible as
a prerequisite of the goals pursued in the development plan. The fact that Argentina's constitutional
government has wide popular backing and democratic
support is a factor of the utmost importance in bol-
stering the basic forces favorable to the development of the nation's economy.

Anyone who has even a passing familiarity with
Argentina is aware that there is not the slightest
trace of xenophobia among its people. Since almost
all the Argentine people are either immigrants or
descendants from immigrants in the first or second
generation, a xenophobic state of mind would be
quite improbable. On the contrary, the people of my
country sincerely admire and obviously support the
technical advances and the creative accomplishments
which foreign assistance has brought to the nation's
economy. Foreigners quickly have a sense of the Argentine desire to extend an unqualified welcome to
anyone who begins to consider settling in the country. Because Argentine society is so fluid, the
process of absorption into the Argentine social
structure is carried out with considerable ease.

In addition to the favorable state of mind with
which the Argentine people look upon the foreigner,
one has also to take into account the nature of the
human and natural resources of the country in order
to be able fully to understand the possibilities for
foreign investments. I cannot cover that subject
fully in the brief compass of this meeting, but I
would like to make some important points.

To begin with, Argentina's human resources are
of the highest quality. One reason for this is the
Argentine educational system. One out of every five
Argentines, including males and females of all ages,

is attending some type of school. Attendance in the
elementary schools for children of appropriate ages
amounts to 88 percent. And the rate of illiteracy
comes to only 8.6 percent; this is one of the lowest
rates in the world and is roughly comparable with the
typical rate of most industrialized countries.

A considerable number of technical schools exist
in the country and each year they graduate numerous
technicians at the intermediate level who are qualified for industrial work. The skill of the specialized industrial workers in Argentina has surprised
foreign managers coming from countries at even higher levels of technological development. Argentina
now has 20,000 working engineers and every year this
number is increased by the output of our universities;
in addition, Argentina educates many other professional groups qualified to participate in the management of enterprises. As evidence of this quality of
our managers and technicians, the United States-owned
firms in Argentina have steadily drawn upon this
group for their personnel requirements.

The standards of nutrition and health of the
Argentine people are comparable to those of most developed countries. The daily food intake amounts to
about 3100 calories, a figure which is only matched
by that of the United States. The medical community
is large in relation to the population and high in
level of competence. All this is reflected in the
fact that the life expectancy of the Argentine
people is sixty-six years at birth, a figure similar
to that prevailing in Western Europe.

About 68 percent of the Argentine people live
in urban areas, and there are a number of cities
with more than 100,000 inhabitants. The most important concentration of population lies in the so-
called "greater Buenos Aires belt," which includes
about 8,000,000 inhabitants. This remarkable concentration of the population has been enlarged at a
particularly rapid rate during the past twenty years
and has brought about a considerable change in consumption habits, with much greater emphasis upon
finished goods. This kind of demand promises to

increase steadily as national income grows, thereby
providing a solid basis for the settlement of added
industry in the country.

At the same time, one must realize that the
cost of labor in my country is calculated about one-
quarter of that in the United States. This does not
mean, of course, that the population's living stand-
ard is as low as one-quarter of the U.S. level; on
the contrary, Argentine living standards are quite
high and promise to grow higher in future years.
What accounts for the relative low cost of labor is
the fact that the price of foodstuffs is so low in
relation to the level that exists in industrialized
countries. This comparative advantage of Argentina
has a special significance in view of the exceptional
opportunities offered by the Latin American Free
Trade Association. The Association, created in 1960,
brings together nine countries with a population of
nearly 170,000,000. Argentina has already achieved
a noticeable increase in exports of manufactures to
the area. And its future prospects are excellent if
one takes into account the country's comparative advantage in costs, its high degree of industrialization, and its high level of technical capacity.

If all these opportunities were left simply to
the capital that could be generated from domestic
savings, the growth rate of Argentina would slacken.
Important as such savings are in Argentina, foreign
capital is also needed. This explains why we attach
so much importance to obtaining foreign capital for
the purpose of sharing in our efforts, so that the
investment levels required by the plan of the Argentine government can be reached.

All this has been said to demonstrate the attractive conditions offered by the Argentine government
to both private and public foreign investment. It
would be hard to imagine another developing economy
in which the possibilities for investment were more
attractive. It is also difficult to imagine another
country in which so high an increase in gross national
product can be obtained by the proper application of
modern planning techniques. Foreign financial help

which supports an appropriate national plan and
which takes cognizance of the special characteristics of the Argentine people will represent the hap-
piest expression of international cooperation. They
will constitute an affirmation of support to a people
who are ready to use all their resources in the
achievement of a task of benefit to the entire South
American continent.

A BRAZILIAN VIEW

by

Helio Jaguaribe

THE CONTROVERSY OVER FOREIGN INVESTMENT

The most striking aspect of the problem of the
contribution of foreign investment to the national
development of countries in our time is the extraordinary divergence of opinion which tends to prevail,
as a rule, between the advocates of foreign investment and its critics in recipient countries. This
controversy goes far beyond the natural opposition
of interests which separates lenders and borrowers.
In disputes between lenders and borrowers, the points
of difference tend to be limited to the conditions of
a credit operation, such as the interest rate, the
risks and guarantees, and the time of maturity. But
there is a general consensus in the world that long-
term credits are indispensible for the national development of the less advanced countries; the need
for credit, therefore, is not the basis for the divergence of opinion.

Why then should the appraisal of foreign investment be so controversial? Are the critics of foreign
investment from the recipient countries systematically uninformed or unjust? Are the defenders of foreign investment systematically biased by a desire for
profit-making or by ideological motivations?

This paper is a brief attempt to analyze the
pros and cons of foreign investment today, in the

Helo Jaguaribe is a Visiting Lecturer in Government at Harvard University. He is the founder and a
member of the Brazilian Institute of Development.

case of Latin America in general and of Brazil in
particular. The study will concentrate on analyzing
the effects of foreign investment, in the promotion
of the national development of less-advanced countries, with special reference to Brazil. Many related problems will be taken as given, such as the
general system of property ownership and property
control, as well as the system of government and public administration. On the other hand, what we shall
mean by the words "national development" is not any
kind of economic growth; it is rather the kind of
growth which leads to maximizing the control of the
nation over its own means and resources. This point
is of great importance. For, as we shall see in the
course of this paper, most of the conflicts over the
role of foreign investment arise over the question of
whether the nation itself is being benefited by the
socio-economic development which is being promoted.

The Arguments Against Foreign Investment

Writing elsewhere in a somewhat broader context,
I attempted to show that the arguments against foreign investment can be systematized in three major
categories: (1) the spoliatory effect, (2) the
balance-of-payments effect, and (3) the colonizing
effect.[1]

The spoliatory effect may stem from two different causes. The first consists of the exaggeration
of the value of the capital contributed by the foreigner. This may be through any of several types of
manipulation, the most usual being the over-estima-
tion of the value of patents, designs and technical
processes. As foreign investments are usually subject to special registration in order to determine
the value of the incoming capital, investors find it
useful to ascribe exaggerated worth to technical elements, especially if the real value is difficult or
impossible to fix. Such practices are especially
attractive when local participation or financing may
also be involved. This first form of the spoliatory
effect of foreign investment, however, is either the
result of manipulation or of loopholes in the law; in

principle, it can be controlled by better methods of
evaluation and registration.

The second form of spoliation which foreign investment can produce, according to its critics, is a
direct consequence of the investment itself and consists of unending accumulations of profits, and of
their total or partial remittance to the home center.
Such criticism is based on the undesirability on the
part of the host country to have profits being accumulated in favor of an external investor after the
investment plus a fair return have already been paid
back. Reinvestment of profits simply adds to the
problem, especially in Latin America where profits on
foreign investment are extremely high. One corollary
of such criticism is that foreign equity investments
are less desirable than long-term loans; even if the
interest payments on such loans are as high as the
net profits of equity investment, the fruits of the
capital cease to be transferred to foreigners once a
loan is fully amortized. Critics accept the counter-
argument that, in the case of equity investment, the
risk of the venture is borne by the foreign investor;
whereas, in the case of foreign loans, it is borne
by the borrower. This difference, they are willing
to concede, justifies a different level of reward.
They insist on the fact, however, that (political
risks apart) the risks of foreign investment are
purely theoretical, given the scale, technique and
organization of foreign operations.

The second argument against foreign investment
is based on its negative effects on the balance of
payments. The argument stresses the fact that, except in the case of a constant increase of new capital inflow, the annual repatriation of capital and
the remittance of profits are larger than the amount
of new capital inflow. Of course, if there were a
constant increase in capital inflow (an assumption
at variance with the statistical facts), the arguments against foreign investment would be weaker
But it is evident that, in any capital investment
based on commercial considerations, the amount corresponding to capital repatriation and profits necessarily surpasses the original investment by the

accumulated amount of net profits. Accordingly, the
critics of foreign investment accept the inevitabil-
ity of an adverse outward flow, insisting at the
same time that debt is the preferred form of investment; debt, they point out, can be limited to the
national capacity for liquidation, whereas the same
cannot be done for foreign equity investment because
of the unpredictability of the decisions concerning
repatriation.

The third argument against foreign investment is
concerned with its colonizing effects. While the
spoliatory criticism emphasizes the excessive cost of
foreign equity investment for the recipient country,
relative to the cost of loans, the colonizing criticism points to the alienating effect of such investment as it tends to transfer to foreigners the control over the productive processes of a country.
Such a transfer has a double consequence. In the
first place, it affects the autonomy of the host
country, by limiting her decision-making capacity in
her own economy. In the second place, the transfer
of control exerts a colonizing effect by depriving
the recipient country of the fruits of the investments in the foreign-controlled sectors.

The importance of the two aspects above is pro-
portionate to the relative importance of foreign investment in the total investment of a country. It
is also a function of the strategic importance of
the sectors under foreign control. It is unnecessary
to point out that, in the case of Latin American
countries, foreign investment occupies a very important position in total investment. What is more,
such investment usually is most prominent in sensi-
tive sectors such as oil in Venezuela and copper in
Chile. The conclusion drawn by the critics of foreign investment is that such investment constitutes
one of the major obstacles to the autonomous and
self-sustained development of Latin America.

The Arguments for Foreign Investment

The points made in favor of foreign investment
may also be summarized under three major headings:

(1) the increase of capacity for national capital
formation; (2) the increase in the productivity of
the economy; and (3) the germinative effect.[2]

The defenders of foreign investment not only
deny the existence of any spoliatory effect (contend-
ing that profits are a necessary stimulus for risk-
ing capital) but they also emphasize the importance
of equity investment in increasing the total capacity
of the recipient country to raise capital. The capacity to borrow is determined, among other conditions, by the pre-existing equity; hence it does no
good to speak of securing capital through loans
rather than equity investment. Underdeveloped countries have, by definition, a low capacity to generate equity investment and, correspondingly, a low
capacity to borrow.

The second argument in favor of foreign equity
investment stresses the fact that its contribution
to the increase in the productivity of the recipient
economy goes beyond the amount of capital provided
to the country, because of the technological advances
brought to the productive process. Foreign investment is usually more than additional investment resulting from external savings. It represents the
utilization of new technical possibilities, bringing
a corresponding increase of productivity. Such favorable effects, for all practical purposes, have to
be brought in from abroad and should be expected to
have a cost in foreign currency. The eventual increase in the deficit of the balance-of-payments resulting from repatriation and profit remittance is
more than compensated by the lasting results of technological improvement, which is the prime engine of
economic development.

The third justification of foreign investment
is founded on its germinative effects. Besides increasing national capital formation and upgrading
the level of productivity, foreign investment exerts
an accelerating and multiplying effect on the economy of the recipient country by opening up new possibilities of investment. Foreign investment tends to
move into the new sectors of the economy, mostly

sectors which are basic for the country's development. Such activities determine the possibility and
induce the appearance of a wider range of related activities. Therefore, foreign investment has a germinative effect; besides its direct production, it opens
up entirely new fields of activity in the economy.

The history of North America is often presented
as the exemplary success story. The unrestricted
welcome given to foreign investment in the nineteenth
century led to the achievement in a few decades of
the most spectacular development ever reached by any
country; this case is offered in painful contrast to
the enduring backwardness of Latin America, which is
said to arise precisely because of its resistance to
foreign investment.

THE FACTS OF THE CASE

A critical appraisal of the opposing sets of
arguments summarized in the preceding section requires an analysis of the underlying facts. Such an
analysis is presented below in a succinct form, having in mind the case of Latin America in general and
Brazil in particular.

Historical Development in Latin America

The history of foreign investment in Latin
America is, in broad terms, divided into distinct
phases by the first World War. Before the war, the
British, and to a lesser extent the French, had been
interested in investing in various sectors of the
infrastructure, such as railways and ports; these
investments were actually a means of carrying out
their more basic purpose, which was to export finished goods to the underdeveloped areas and to import raw materials and primary products from those
areas. Creating or improving transport and communications facilities was a pre-requisite for a substantial expansion of British (or French) trade.

After the first World War, however, the British
interest steadily declined, as the United Kingdom

preferred to concentrate its comparatively diminishing business influence in the Commonwealth area.
Since that time, American interest in Latin America
has been constantly increasing, both in terms of
trade and of capital investment; today, when one
speaks of foreign capital in that area, one is speak-
ing of American capital for all practical purposes.

U.S. investments in Latin America before the
second World War were mainly concentrated in oil
(Venezuela), mining (Chile and Peru), manufacturing
(Argentina, Brazil, Uruguay, Chile and Mexico), public utilities and trade. From $1,069 millions in
1908, this investment rose to $2,406 millions in
1919 and to $4,101 millions in 1937, including equi-
ty capital and loans.[3] By 1933, U.S. private <u>direct</u>
industrial investment (including oil refining) in
the southern countries of Latin America amounted to
more than $230 million, spread through 66 branch
plants, most of them installed from the middle 20's
onward.[4] (Direct investment here and elsewhere
means equity investment accompanied by management
and control.)

The American tendency to invest in Latin America
increased after the second World War. At the end of
1961, Latin America was the second highest area of
concentration of United States direct investments--
greater than Europe and surpassed only by Canada.
It was not until 1962 that United States direct investment in Europe became higher than in Latin America; by that year, as shown in Table 1, Europe came
to represent 24.0% and Latin America, 22.6% of United States total direct investment abroad. At the
end of 1963, United States direct investment in
Latin America had taken a pattern, by fields of application and country, as shown in Table 2.

Effects on Latin American
Balance of Payments

One of the most serious weaknesses of Latin
American economies in recent years has been the per-
sistent deficit in their balance of payments; this
is due, as has been pointed out by the studies of

the Economic Commission for Latin America, to structural causes. Among these causes, the two most relevant are (1) the combined effect of the insufficient
growth of the volume of the exports, mainly because
of the insufficient increase in the international demand for Latin American traditional goods; and (2)
the continued deterioration of Latin America's terms
of trade. On the other hand, the Latin American
balance-of-payment deficit is also due to the deficit arising out of capital transactions. In the
period 1951-60, for instance, in spite of the surplus in their balance of trade, Latin American countries have accumulated a balance-of-payment deficit
on current account of the order of $9 billion, as
shown in Table 3.

The role played by foreign capital in creating
the deficit in the Latin American payments position
may be seen in Table 4. While the inflow of direct
investment in the period 1951-60 has been only $6.2
billion, the outflow of profits and capital repatriation has exceeded $10 billion. Even considering the
movement of loans and interest, the difference between the total inflow and outflow of capital and
related payments continues to be negative.

Investment and Reinvestment

In recent years, United States private investment in Latin America has manifested an increasing
preference for portfolio investment at the expense
of direct investment, as indicated by Table 5.
While direct investment decreased from 76.3% in 1958
to 70.0% in 1963 of total private investment, portfolio investment registered an increase from 10.2%
to 13.9% for the respective years.

The difference between portfolio and direct investment, for the recipient country, is important
from a number of different viewpoints. It suffices,
for the purpose of this analysis, to point out two.
The first concerns control and management; in principle, control and management are retained by the recipient country in the case of portfolio investment,
but they are transferred to the foreign investors in

the case of direct investment. The second relates
to the policy on profits; these tend to be remitted
to the home country of portfolio investors, while
they are reinvested in substantial part by direct
investors. The result of these tendencies is that
portfolio investors tend to interfere little in control and management, but they tend to press more
heavily on the balance of payments. Direct investment is oriented to control and management by the
investing firms, but at the same time these firms
are less interested in bringing profits home than
in increasing the value of their investment by constant reinvestment. The fact that U.S. private investment is predominantly of the direct kind explains why reinvestment has been larger than new investment in Latin America (Table 6).

Foreign Investment in Brazil

United States direct investment in Brazil in
1963 represented about 80% of the total foreign investment in that country and amounted to absolute
amounts of $1,128 million, as shown in Table 7. The
table also shows that, in the five-year period ter-
minating in 1963, United States direct investment in
Brazil had built up steadily.

In spite of the increasing amount of United
States investments, the Brazilian payments balance
as related to foreign capital movements, as is the
case with Latin America as a whole, is strongly negative. In an earlier study of this subject, I indicated that, according to the annual report of Banco
do Brasil, the deficit for the fifteen-year period
1940-1956 amounted to about $900 million.[5] The fore-
cast for the three-year period 1963-65, according to
the Triennial Plan of Economic and Social Development of 1962, presented the following figures in
millions of United States dollars:

Profits and interest	-$ 500	
Capital repayments	- 1,285	
Outflow		-$1,785
New equity investments	310	
New loans	960	
Inflow		1,270
BALANCE		- 515

According to the same pattern which was earlier
noted in the case of Latin America as a whole, foreign investments in Brazil are substantially formed
by reinvestment of profits.   In its first general
survey of foreign investment in 1951, Banco do Brasil
concluded that, of the 28.9 billion cruzeiros of foreign investment then registered, 14.8 billion cruzeiros (using an exchange rate of one United States
dollar to 18.82 cruzeiros) were reinvestments while
only 14.1 billion were original investments.   Aristoteles Moura, basing his analysis on data in the
Survey of Current Business of the United States Department of Commerce of 1954, calculates that from
1946 to 1951, 40% of the total United States direct
investment in Brazil was reinvested profit.   In the
two years following, reinvested profits went up to
62% of total investment.[6]

A CRITICAL APPRAISAL

Taking in account the data presented above, it
is now possible to attempt a critical appraisal of
the controversy on foreign investment which has been
summarized in the first section of the paper.

It would not be unfair, in starting this discussion, to point out that the burden of proof should
be borne by the defenders rather than by the critics
of foreign investment.   This is so because, contrary
to what is often alleged by advocates of foreign investment, Latin American countries were open without
restriction to alien capital from the time of their
independence until the Great Depression of the nine-
teen-thirties.   If the Latin American countries re-
main retarded in the second half of the present century, when even the old immobile societies of Asia
are making great leaps forward and are catching up
technologically, the reason cannot be ascribed to
Latin American hostility toward foreign capital; instead, it should be acknowledged that among the
causes of Latin American backwardness is the fact
that foreign capital has been unable to achieve in
the South what it has done in the North.

It is because of the difference in conditions
between the South and the North that the controversy
on foreign capital remains open in Latin America.
Neither the natural resources nor the social organization of Latin America has been as favorable to its
development as was the case in the United States.
The foreign capital which came to the United States
in the first three quarters of the nineteenth century
came at a time when such investment was in the hands
of individuals or limited firms; in the case of direct investment, these owners followed the successful path of their money, immigrating to the United
States and so automatically nationalizing their
assets.   The foreign capital which became interested
in Latin America, however, came in a later historical
period.   The investors were no longer the small and
medium sized firm belonging to individuals inclined
to immigrate; they were large international corporations, opening branches that would stay forever attached to or controlled by the parent companies.
This, then, is the kind of foreign investment with
which Latin America has had to contend.

Spoliatory Effect vs. Increase
in National Investment

Both sides are right when they say that foreign
investment tends to feed upon itself and that foreign
investment increases total domestic capital formation.
Data cited earlier show that about one-half of foreign
investment in Latin America is formed by the reinvestment of profits.   It is no less indisputable that both
investment and reinvestment are contributing to increase the domestic product.

The problem to discuss, therefore, is not an absolute negative or positive value of foreign investment but its relative value in the conditions in
which it takes place.   This depends basically on
answers to the two following questions:

(1) What better alternative use for the
national development of the country could
be given to the factors and opportunities
that are employed by foreign investment?

(2) What, if any, are the negative effects resulting from the fact that the investment
is foreign and what is the balance between
such effects and the domestic product
generated by the investment?

The first question presents, at the same time,
a problem of availability of resources and of their
best allocation. If national resources are not too
abundant or could easily be better allocated, it is
probable that a better alternative use might be
given to factors and opportunities employed by foreign investment. If these conditions are not satis-
fied, it is more probable that foreign investment is
an alternative for doing nothing; in that case, what
should be considered is the balance between the negative effect which might arise from the fact that the
investment is foreign, and the increase of the domestic product caused by the investment.

In its studies of the need for foreign capital
to complement domestic savings in Latin America, the
Economic Commission for Latin America has come to
the following conclusions:[7]

(a) Even at the present unsatisfactory levels
and conditions of taxation, Latin American
domestic savings would be sufficient to finance
the region's development, were it not for the
deterioration of the region's terms of trade.
Terms of trade deterioration subtracts a sum
annually from the gross product of the area
which varied, in the period 1950-54, between
0.3% to 0.6%. In the five years succeeding,
the amount grew, varying from 1.9% to 4.0%
annually.

(b) Net external financing in the period from
1950 to 1960 contributed an amount varying annually from 0.5% to 3.1% of the area's gross product. This has meant that external financing,
which represented 6% of the area's gross capital formation in 1950, went up to 10% by the
end of the period. In the latter part of that
period, from 1955 to 1960, the external

financing becomes more important when compared
to net national savings; in that period, such
financing came to 19% of net national savings
for Latin America.

The necessity for external financing, however,
presents a more complicated picture because of the
deficit in the balance of payments of Latin American
countries. If external financing is to be used,
both to compensate for the balance-of-payments defi-
cits and to complement domestic savings, it can be
estimated that, for the period up to 1970, about
$3 billion annually will be needed by the Latin
American countries in external financing; only then
would it be possible for the area to pay its external debts and to maintain the minimum annual per
capita growth of 2.5%. Investments in such amounts
greatly exceed the $2 billion annual goal of the
Alliance for Progress and are many times larger than
the projection of foreign capital inflow for the
same period, estimated between $400 and $500 million
annually.

Balance-of-payment Drain vs.
Productivity Increase

Data on the negative effect of foreign investments on the balance of payments are irrefutable.
As we pointed out earlier, foreign investments will
necessarily have an adverse effect on the balance of
payments because profits or interest will have to be
repatriated in addition to the original principal;
the only possible exception is the case in which the
capital inflow increases constantly, but this would
only aggravate the other adverse effects of foreign
investment.

On the other hand, it is not true, as has so
often been alleged, that foreign capital makes more
than a proportional contribution to the increase of
productivity. The allegation is founded on the consideration that the technological improvements which
accompany foreign equity investment would not be
available if the investment took the form of loans.
To have the technique besides the money, a borrower

would have to pay an additional price; but the direct
investor, in his own interest, brings with him the
best available technique.

The first qualification relevant to such an argument concerns the kind of technique involved, in
relation to the stage of development of the recipient country. Much of the technology used by foreign
investment, for countries in the stage of development of the principal countries of Latin America, is
already widely known. In those cases in which the
technology is not widely known, the reasons are economic rather than technical.

Techniques which genuinely constitute technical
innovation are never imparted by foreign investors
to the recipient countries. If the technique is of
the kind that can be actually transmitted, it tends
to be protected by the utmost secrecy; Brazil's recent experience with industrialization confirms that
foreign-owned firms make a secret of techniques whenever possible in order to prolong technical dependence. On the other hand, if the process or knowledge is dependent on a program of ongoing research,
the recipient country never acquires the control of
the technique simply because it is constantly being
used and improved by the foreign-owned firm.

It cannot be said, therefore, that the technical advantages of foreign investment, except in
special cases, give it a value greater than the net
cost of the technique to the country. On the contrary, technical and organizational improvements
tend to be possible only when the initiative is taken
and controlled by the developing country. This can
be done by giving minority participations to foreign
capital and securing appropriate stipulations about
know-how transmission. More often, it can be done
simply by training local people and developing local
institutions. For, although technological innovation is zealously kept secret by business concerns,
foreign universities and cultural institutions are
usually quite ready to provide what they know; and
their knowledge will carry the recipient country a
considerable way.

Colonizing Effect vs. Germinative Effect

The facts lend full support to the colonizing
argument--even more, perhaps, than what is immediately apparent in the relevant statistics. National development should not be confused with simple per
capita growth of national income or domestic product.
The socio-economic development of a country is the
development of her modes of social organization and
production; this development must be measured not
only, or even primarily, in terms of the simple op-
timization of the use of her natural and human resources, but rather in terms of the extent to which
the nation increases her capacity for autonomy and
independence. Mere economic development of a nation,
if it is not accompanied by an increasing national
command over conditions, results ultimately in bene-
fiting some other country and leads to the final dis-
solution of the nation that is being developed.

The arguments concerning the germinative effect
of foreign investment are relevant to investments as
a whole, rather than specifically to investments of
foreign origin. All investments have some multipli-
cative effect, especially when their scale, efficiency, and opportunity of application are providing the
conditions for increased economic expansion by others.

We noted earlier that the colonizing effect of
foreign investment depends upon the stage of development of a country and is a function of her alternative possibilities of investment. As far as backward traditional countries are concerned, these alternative possibilities usually cannot develop without external pressure; the oligarchies which control
such countries as a rule tend to prevent any other
alternative. In those cases, the colonizing effect
of foreign investment plays a positive historical
role.

In the transitional and take-off stages, however,
a country needs to devote her maximum efforts to the
optimum allocation of her resources and, at the same
time, needs to define and to consolidate her national
identity. At these stages, colonizing effects tend

to divert scarce resources from their proper use and
to dissipate constructive opportunities and weaken
useful social forces. At the same time, as the Latin
American case illustrates so well, these stages tend
to be the ones in which external financing is most
needed.

It should be finally observed that, in the latter stages of development, when the process is far
advanced, foreign investment loses its colonizing
effect. As long as indigenous capital is predominant,
foreign investment in the advanced countries tends to
make a positive contribution by maintaining internal
competition and stimulating innovation.

CONCLUSIONS AND POLICY IMPLICATIONS

General Principles

The role of foreign capital in the promotion of
national development can be summarized in a few basic
propositions.

First, foreign investment increases domestic
capital formation, but it does so at a cost. In
balance-of-payment terms, it places a liability on
the country equal to the amount of capital to be repatriated plus transferable profits to be generated
by the foreign investment until its liquidation is
completed. In factor use terms, it excludes the possibility of giving better alternative use to the factors and opportunities employed by the foreign investment. In power terms, it transfers the decision-
making and capital accumulation provided by the investment to those who control and operate it; at the
same time, such investment prevents national capital
from using the factors and opportunities that are
being employed by the foreign investment.

Second, the balance between advantages and dis-
advantages of foreign investment to the recipient
country turns on a number of judgments. Has the increased burden on the balance of payments led to a
better employment of the nation's assets for her

national development? Has the investment provided a
better use for the factors and opportunities used by
the investment than would have been the case if the
investment has not been made? Was there some alternative way of securing foreign savings with fewer
negative effects in terms of balance of payments and
of national autonomy and self-sufficiency? Could
more important development goals have been obtained
with the same amount of foreign investment?

In policy terms, these issues suggest a number
of major points.

First and foremost is the fact that foreign
capital should be planned as a marginal complement
of the desired domestic capital formation. In the
case of Brazil, as in the case of Latin America in
general, the practice more often than not has been
the opposite. Because of the relative ease in mobilizing foreign capital, that source has been overused
despite the direct and indirect costs of the policy.
Domestic savings have been held down because of the
internal political resistance to change in the status
quo, especially with regard to measures which redis-
tribute income and increase taxation. The same political resistance has tended to generate a poor allocation of resources. It is self-defeating to try to
overcome a shortage of domestic savings by the increased use of foreign capital. People in Latin
America must be bluntly forced to face the choice between some temporary additional sacrifices for national development or stagnation under foreign domination. If they choose the latter, they will ultimately be obliged to make much worse sacrifices per-
manently and without any purpose or result.

The second major point of policy is that Latin
American countries need to establish a general approach which will assure predominance of their national capital. For that purpose, they need to define what sectors will be reserved for state monopoly
for national security reasons (such as petroleum in
Brazil); what sectors will be reserved for control
by national capital (such as the infrastructural and
basic sectors); and what areas will be kept free for

any investor fulfilling the general conditions set
out in the national development plan.

This delimitation of investment possibilities
would serve to orient both investors and government
authorities. It is also an indispensable prerequisite for the integration of Latin America. As the
integration of Latin America proceeds, it is necessary that prospective foreign investors should clearly understand which sectors of the broadened Latin
American market will be kept open for them and under
what conditions. Integrating Latin America without
the clearest possible settlement of this question
would amount to opening the most advanced areas of
the region to foreign domination and would result in
the irreversible loss of regional autonomy and self-
sufficiency.

The third point of policy relates to the use of
loans versus the use of equity investments. Given
the level of socio-economic development already
achieved by Latin America as a whole and particularly of its most important countries, long-term loans
should be given preference over foreign equity investment. This preference arises partly from the
balance-of-payment implications and partly from the
colonizing consequences of equity investments as compared with loans. Any balance-of-payment "solution"
based on increased equity investment would be nothing more than a temporary palliative. Latin America's
deficit is of a structural nature and cannot be cor-
rected in one or two years; it requires a long-term
plan for its balancing. The plan involves a re-
shaping of the structure of the international trade
of the area, leading to an increase and diversifica-
tion of exports and to a decrease of imports through
a substantial expansion in the internal production
of capital goods.

In those cases in which foreign investment
would be required, according to the criteria indicated above, the form to be preferred would be that
of joint ventures, assuring initial or ultimate
majority control for the Latin American partners.
Perpetual foreign control over important sectors of

the economy of the host country is not compatible
with the national emancipation of Latin American
countries. Colonial forms of foreign investment,
such as oil in Venezuela and copper in Chile, are
undesirable. Wherever such investments exist, negotiations should be launched which are aimed at trans-
ferring control to domestic national capital on mu-
tually acceptable terms and in the shortest possible
period of time.

Studies undertaken by the Inter-American Development Bank, by the Economic Commission for Latin
America, and by other entities point to the conclusion that there is an historical deadline facing
Latin America if it is ever to achieve independent
self-sustained development. Tentatively, the year
1980 has been suggested as the time when the minimal
conditions for autonomous development should be at-
tained by Latin America. These studies emphasize
that the economic, political and social differences
between Latin America and the developed countries
(especially the United States) will become so wide,
so fundamental and so irreversible that Latin American nations will lose their capacity to function as
the socio-political framework of their own societies.

Increasing dependence on alien developed countries, particularly the United States, together with
increasing internal poverty and unrest, would leave
the Latin American peoples with the choice between
permanent foreign domination and internal revolution.
This alternative is already visible in the Caribbean
area, where the countries have lost their individual
viability and are not being allowed, by the combined
action of their own internal oligarchies and the external intervention of the United States, to form a
larger autonomous community. What is happening today in the Caribbean is likely to happen in less
than two decades in the major Latin American countries if they do not achieve minimal conditions of
autonomous self-sustained development.

Autonomy, therefore, is the crucial question of
socio-economic development and is both a condition
for its promotion and an objective for its achieve-

ment.   A certain measure of international cooperation and interdependence will always be required.
But hand in hand with this cooperation must go the
actual control by a country of her own decision-
making processes.   On an economic plane, this means
that she must own her own factories, develop her own
techniques and manage her own processes of production.

Footnotes

1.   Helio Jaguaribe, O Nacionalismo na Atuali-
dade Brasileira, Instituto Superior de Estudos
Brasileiros (ISEB) (Rio de Janeiro, 1958), p. 168.

2.   Ibid., p. 175.

3.   Data quoted by Aristoteles Moura in Capitais
Estrangeiros no Brasil, 2nd ed. (Sao Paulo: Ed.
Brasiliense, 1960) from U. N. Foreign Capital in
Latin America (New York: United Nations, 1955), p.
154.

4.   See Dudley M. Phelps, Migration of Industry
to South America (New York: McGraw-Hill, 1936).

5.   See the 1953 report of Banco do Brasil, especially pp. 170-171, for a more detailed presenta-
tion of the data presented here and below.

6.   Aristoteles Moura, op. cit., p. 43.

7.   Economic Commission on Latin America, The
Role of External Financing in the Economic Develop-
ment of Latin America in Postwar Period (Mar del
Plata, Argentina: United Nations, 1963).

TABLE 1

U.S. Direct Investment Abroad
(millions of dollars)

Area	1959	1960	1961	1962	1963[a]
All areas	29,827	32,778	34,667	37,226	40,645
Latin America	8,120	8,387	8,236	8,424	8,657
Canada	10,310	11,198	11,602	12,133	13,016
Other Western Hemisphere	768	884	954	1,050	1,218
Europe	5,323	6,681	7,742	8,930	10,351
Africa	833	925	1,064	1,271	1,423
Asia	2,237	2,291	2,477	2,500	2,784
Oceania	879	994	1,108	1,271	1,463
International	1,357	1,418	1,485	1,647	1,732

[a]Preliminary

Sources: 1959, 1960 data from Table 2 of Survey of
          Current Business, XLII, No. 8 (August,
          1962), 22.
          1961, 1962, 1963 data from Table 2 of Survey
          of Current Business, XLIV, No. 8 (Aug-
          ust, 1964), 10.

TABLE 2

U.S. Direct Investment in Latin America, 1963[a]

(millions of dollars)

Country	Total	Mining & Smelting	Petroleum	Manufacturing	Public Utility	Trade	Other Industries
All areas	40,645	3,350	13,698	14,890	2,051	3,305	3,351
Latin America	8,657	1,093	3,094	2,103	710	881	776
Argentina	828	(b)	(b)	454	(b)	38	336
Brazil	1,128	30	60	663	190	147	38
Chile	768	503	(b)	27	(b)	15	223
Colombia	465	(b)	245	120	27	52	19
Mexico	907	116	66	503	25	93	104
Peru	448	240	56	64	21	41	27
Uruguay	51	(b)	(b)	20	(b)	6	24
Venezuela	2,807	(b)	2,166	202	37	185	218

[a]Preliminary

[b]Combined in other industries

Source: Table 2, Survey of Current Business, XLIV, No. 8 (August, 1964), 10.

TABLE 3

Latin American Balance of Payments
on Current Account, 1951-1960
(millions of dollars)

Period	Exports f.o.b.	Imports			Investment Income			On current account
		Merchandise f.o.b.	Services net[a]	Total	Direct investments	Interest on loan & others	Total	
1951-55	38,493.5	-34,662.4	-2,196.1	-36,858.5	-4,458.7	-503.1	-4,961.8	-3,326.8
1956-60[b]	42,850.1	-39,756.4	-2,153.9	-41,210.3	-5,604.6	-990.0	-6,594.6	-5,654.8
1951-60	81,343.6	-74,418.8	-4,350.0	-78,068.8	-10,063.3	-1,493.1	-11,556.4	-8,981.6

[a]Services include tourism and private gifts in addition to other services.
[b]Data for 1960 exclude Cuba.

Source: Economic Commission for Latin America, The Economic Development of Latin America in the Postwar Period (Mar del Plata, Argentina: United Nations, 1963), Table 70.

TABLE 4

Balance of Payments Effects of Capital Movement
and Capital Servicing Payments in Latin America
(millions of dollars)

Period	Receipts			Payments			Balance
	Direct investment	Net total of loans & other movements	Inflow	Profits & repatriation	Interest on loan & others	Outflow	
1951-55	1,715.5	1,032.5	2,748.0	- 4,458.7	- 503.1	- 4,961.8	-2,213.8
1955-60	4,529.4	1,674.0	6,203.4	- 5,604.6	- 990.0	- 6,594.6	- 391.2
1951-60	6,244.9	2,706.5	8,951.4	-10,063.3	-1,493.1	-11,556.4	-2,605.0

Source: Economic Commission for Latin America, The Economic Development of Latin America in the Postwar Period (Mar del Plata, Argentina: United Nations, 1963), Tables 70 and 76.

TABLE 5

U.S. Private Investment in Latin America by Type
(millions of dollars)

Type	1958	1959	1960	1961[a]	1962	1963[b]
Total	10,154	10,749	11,501	11,637	12,111	12,368
Long-term	8,790	9,311	9,872	9,865	10,185	10,380
Direct	7,751	8,098	8,387	8,255	8,424	8,657
Portfolio	1,039	1,213	1,485	1,610	1,761	1,723
Short-term	1,364	1,438	1,629	1,722	1,926	1,988

[a]Data for Cuba omitted for 1961 and subsequent years.

[b]Preliminary

Sources: 1958 from Table 7 of Survey of Current
           Business, XL, No. 9 (September, 1960), 24.

           1959 from Table 7 of Survey of Current
           Business, XLI, No. 8 (August, 1961), 26.

           1960 from Table 7 of Survey of Current
           Business, XLII, No. 8 (August, 1962), 32.

           1961 from Table 9 of Survey of Current
           Business, XLIII, No. 8 (August, 1963), 22.

           1962, 1963 from Table 12 of Survey of
           Current Business, XLIV, No. 8 (August,
           1964), 24.

TABLE 6

Investment, Reinvestment and Repatriation of United States
Private Direct Investments in Latin America

Year	New In-vestment	Rein-vestment	Total In-vestment & Rein-vestment	Repatri-ation	Net In-vestment	Reinvest-ment as % of Total
		(Millions of Dollars)				
1950	47	105	152	36	116	69
1951	209	276	485	38	447	57
1952	324	305	629	44	585	48
1953	93	172	265	43	222	65
TOTAL	673	858	1,531	161	1,370	56

Source: Economic Commission for Latin America, International Cooperation in a Latin American Development Policy (New York: United Nations, 1954), Table 3.

TABLE 7

U.S. Private Direct Investment in Brazil
(millions of dollars)

1951	828
1960	953
1961	1,006
1962	1,084
1963[a]	1,128

[a] 1963 figures are preliminary estimates.

Sources: 1959-60 from Table 2 of Survey of Current
            Business, XLII, No. 8 (August, 1962), 22;
            1961-1963, from Table 2 of Survey of
            Current Business, XLIV, No. 8 (August,
            1964), 10.

AN INTERPRETATION OF THE MEXICAN VIEW

by

Raymond Vernon

Mexico's history of economic development is a tale of high drama--of authentic drama filled with episodes of treachery and heroism, blood and tears. It is drama punctuated also with incidents of sad comic-relief, such as the brief improbable era of the Emperor Maximilian and his Carlotta. But even the comic episodes of Mexico are touched with blood.

It is no great wonder, therefore, that modern Mexico customarily speaks of itself in terms that have an accent of unwonted hyperbole. Nor is it altogether surprising that the body of Mexican commentary on its national history is somewhat more self-indulgent in the handling of historical facts than are most national commentaries. Villains, in the telling of Mexican history, tend to be unambiguous villains; heroes bear unsullied escutcheons to the grave.

In most accounts of Mexican history, the foreign investor is cast in the role of villain. Out of the oversimplification that passion and patriotism demand, the foreign investor emerges--along with the landlord and the Church--as one of the enduring symbols of economic exploitation of the Mexican people.

But all things change. Mexico is now half a century from its revolution. Its early need for a few unambiguous villain-figures is now declining. As the country's visible accomplishments grow, the self-assurance of its people increases too. A growing sense of self-assurance and a growing capacity for self-examination, one hopes, go hand-in-hand. It may be that the Mexican view of the foreign

investor will prove increasingly complex in the future, reflecting a parallel change in the investor's
role in the extraordinary country. For the present,
however, one still must turn to history in order to
acquire the beginnings of an understanding of the
Mexican view.

THE FORMATIVE YEARS

There is no satisfactory place to begin a story
of this sort. Historical events build upon those
that went before, in a seamless continuity.

The year 1876, however, marks an historical
turning point of sorts. By that year, Mexico had
endured half a century of unbelievable turmoil. During that half-century, Mexico had established and un-
seated several dozen presidents. It had acquired
and sloughed off the French-imposed imperial reign.
It had seen some changes, such as the transfer of
some of the Church lands and much of the Indian
lands to speculators and adventurers. But it had
seen almost no foreign investment, except perhaps in
a few mines and plantations and in a pitiful 400
miles of railroad track between Vera Cruz and Mexico
City.

In 1876, the reign of Porfirio Diaz begins. The
story of that era has been told and retold in Mexican literature. Almost invariably, Diaz is cast in
the role of the total villain. (There is, however,
a small dissenting tradition which casts him in the
role of an unsung hero, an equally improbable cast-
ing.)

Porfirio Diaz brought an iron peace to Mexico.
Using a combination of force and persuasion, he managed to pull together a coalition of landlords,
brigands, local politicians, and modern intellectuals in the creation of Mexico's first effective national government. Neither the peace nor the effec-
tiveness of the Porfirio era is offensive in modern
Mexican eyes. What is thoroughly offensive, however,
is the philosophy and execution of the economic de-

velopment program of that curious period.

In order to spare those readers who are already
familiar with the Porfirian era, I shall touch only
lightly on the main outlines of the philosophy. But
other readers will find it useful to bear these outlines well in mind. Briefly, the intellectuals
among the Diaz administrators were a product of
their times; and their times were the late 19th century when the rationalism of Spencer and Darwin had
taken strong hold on the educated mind. In the Mexican setting of the time, Diaz' lieutenants sought to
apply a series of unforgivable propositions. They
took cognizance of the cultural inferiority of the
Indian civilization and the productive inadequacy of
the people it had nurtured; until development and
growth lifted them out of the dust, according to the
theory of the times, the Indians could not be expected to do much more than work as common labor in the
fields and mines. Concurrently, the Diaz lieutenants accepted the proposition of the innate superior-
ity of the European culture and the contribution
which that culture could make to Mexico. To achieve
development in the country, they gave the freest possible reign to the foreigner and pushed the Indian
aside whenever he got in the way.

In concrete terms, the Porfirian approach led
to the dramatic extension of a land tenure policy
which Mexico's great Jeffersonian president, Benito
Juarez, had mistakenly initiated--a policy of the
expropriation of land held by peasant farmers, wherever a shadow existed on their title. (In a country
which had lived in continuous turmoil for the
seventy-five years preceding Porfirio Diaz, there
were few landholdings without such a shadow.) And
the Porfirian regime invited foreigners to exploit
the vast land tracts and to develop the plantations,
mining enterprises, oil fields, railroads, and public utilities which the country could support.

Foreigners responded to the opportunities of
the Porfirian era in a number of different ways.

Some foreigners migrated to Mexico; though

maintaining their original citizenship and their
home sources of capital during the first generation
or two, many British, French, German, and Spanish
entrepreneurs came to Mexico to set up textile mills,
tobacco plants and breweries; others developed cotton, sugar, coffee, and henequen plantations, sometimes with related processing plants.

A larger group of foreigners, however, partici-
pated more vicariously in Mexico's development. The
mining and petroleum companies of Britain and the
United States set up their subsidiaries wherever rich
supplies of raw materials could be found. The investors of the United States and Europe bought extraordinary quantities of Mexican government debt and of
Mexican railroad and public utility securities. By
1911, we are told, foreigners had investments in
Mexico totalling $2 billion, a figure said to ac-
count for about two-thirds of aggregate Mexican investment outside of the agriculture and handicraft
industries. By that year, therefore, when Mexico's
decade of revolution begins, foreigners had come to
control so high a proportion of Mexico's wealth that
the proportion may have set all-time records for any
country claiming political independence.

The Porfirian period contributed powerfully to
the deep-seated hostility of Mexico toward the foreign investor. Ironically, however, it also generated many of the indispensable conditions for the
sustained growth of the Mexican economy that was to
follow.

The modernizing impact of the Porfirian era occurred in various ways. One of these--perhaps the
most dramatic--was the building of 15,000 miles of
railroad lines. Because the lines were principally
developed as adjuncts of the mining industry, they
were of many incompatible shapes and sizes; and
while some areas of Mexico were served by closely
parallel facilities, others were wholly neglected.
Still, one does not need constructive intentions to
do constructive work. Once the railroads were built,
they served purposes for which they had not origin-
ally been intended. By 1911, mineral products

accounted for only half of the freight carried on
these roads. Another 23 percent of that freight consisted of agricultural products; forest products accounted for 12 percent; general merchandise for 11
percent; and livestock for 4 percent.

That Mexico benefitted greatly from the investment of foreigners was suggested by various other
indexes. During the period that Mexico became an
export-oriented economy, from 1880 to 1910, the
world prices of raw materials were going up rapidly--
much more rapidly, as nearly as one can tell, than
the prices of finished products. One major exception to the pattern was silver, which was being de-
monetized at the time by the United States. As a
result, Mexico's imports, measured in physical terms,
were fully able to keep pace with her phenomenally
expanding exports. Nor should one suppose that the
imports were chiefly gaudy baubles for the rich.
Gaudy baubles there must have been; but, in the main,
imports consisted of a variety of mundane products,
ranging from food and clothing to industrial raw materials and capital goods.

The opening up of Mexico had many other modernizing effects upon its economy, some subtle, some
very obvious. Both the mining communities and the
cities began to bid away agricultural labor from the
haciendas and the Indian villages. In addition,
there were some rather dramatic shifts and reorgani-
zations of agriculture itself--shifts which on the
whole seemed to push Mexico toward increased agricultural efficiency. Cotton cultivation, for instance,
loosened its locational tie to the textile industry.
Instead of remaining concentrated in the relatively
inferior growing areas close to the Vera Cruz-Mexico
City axis, cotton cultivation moved northward to the
irrigated lands of Nuevo Leon and other northern
states. The data of the period show that the piti-
fully low agricultural wage level was subject to
some upward pressure, that the relative size of the
agricultural labor force declined somewhat, and that
there were widespread complaints about the shortage
of agricultural labor--all salutary developments in
welfare terms.

The various changes which Diaz brought to Mexico
also had major consequences for the development of a
modern state. Although the foreign mines were oriented principally to export, some 155 "metallurgical
establishments" had come into existence by the year
1906. In most cases, these works were established
very close to the mine sites, suggesting a classical
"forward linkage" relationship. In addition, the industrial production indexes of the Porfirian period,
such as they are, showed phenomenal increases in the
production of the infant industries of that day.
Finally, the nation's population censuses showed a
sharp rise in the tiny corps of professional managerial, and technical men who were already forming the
nucleus of a modern state.

But man does not live by fact alone; certainly
not by the narrow type of economic fact which de-
scribes the accomplishments of the Porfirian era.
What was done had been achieved at a high price. In
the process, the Indian populations had been cruelly
abused and neglected. The nation's resources had
been placed in the control of foreigners. National
pride had been deeply and painfully offended. It is
not surprising that, as the years went on, the collective Mexican memory and the collective Mexican
interpretation emphasized the negative aspects of
the period.

THE HARDENING MOLD

The 1920's

Foreigners who had the poor judgment to lend
money to the Porfirian government probably suffered
considerable losses from the decade of the Revolution. But foreigners who invested in railroads, public utilities, mines and petroleum managed to avoid
catastrophe. The mines and the oil fields were located in isolated enclaves, for the most part; and
these could be defended from violence either by
force or by tribute. The utilities at this stage of
Mexico's development were largely in urban locations;
and there was no great incentive on the part of

urban dwellers to cut off their own source of light
and power. The railroads, though run down and
abused by the peripatetic armies of the Revolution,
were not easily destroyed.

The result was that the infrastructure acquired
under the somewhat unusual conditions of the Porfirian era survived to serve Mexico's post-Revolutionary
governments. I have speculated elsewhere that the
kind of national government which emerged after the
bloody Revolutionary decade might not have been possible without the existence of the railroad grid. The
deep-seated localism of Mexico, which had temporarily
been overcome in the Porfirian period by a system
based on force, bribery and exploitation, now had to
be replaced by a system containing a somewhat larger
element of popular consent. But in the conditions of
Mexico in the 1920's, consent was more readily forth-
coming from the aging generals and caciques of Mexico's remote mountains and sparsely settled plains if
the government in Mexico City carried a large and
credible stick. The railroad grid was indispensable
to the Federal Government in presenting that impres-
sion to would-be rebels.

As Mexico was pacified, the foreign-owned enterprises once more were drawn into business. Metal
producers moderately expanded their output in Mexico
during the 1920's, responding to the world's increased demand for nonferrous metals. Oil producers
pushed their output to an all-time peak of 193 million barrels in 1921, then allowed their production
to decline throughout the rest of the decade.

It is to be noted that there was a certain subdued quality in the reaction of the raw material
foreign investors in this period. And there was
good reason for them to feel a trifle subdued. The
new Constitution of the Mexican Revolution, conceived in open convention in 1917, carried overtones
of trouble for the foreign investor, especially the
investor who based his activities upon Mexico's un-
replenishable subsoil resources. Title to the
wealth of the subsoil, according to the new Constitution's provisions, resided in the state, and that

title was inalienable; hence, concessionaires who
mined the subsoil seemed to hold their title only on
the sufferance of the state. On top of this, the
right of foreigners to hold property in Mexico was
circumscribed in a number of specific ways. Land on
the shores or borders of Mexico, for instance, could
not be owned by foreign investors.

There is probably nothing that is totally inexor-
able in the broad sweep of history. But there did
seem to be a certain element of inexorability in the
steps that followed the era of the 1920's, leading
to the Mexican recapture of the ownership of the oil
resources, the public utilities, and much of the land
previously in foreign hands. To get the flavor of
the process, to appreciate how much of it was the consequence of large historical forces and how much of
it the consequence of accidents of personality and
timing, it may be worthwhile to recount briefly some
of the salient events.

The Nationalization of Oil

The basic problem of the foreign oil companies
and the Mexican government in the post-Revolutionary
period was to substitute a new relationship for one
which, though appropriate in its time, had simply
been rendered obsolete by events. Neither side was
free to search for that relationship with any degree
of objectivity.

Picture the situation of the oil companies.
After 1911, they had been living by their wits, partly by politicking intensively with a stream of in-
secure provisional governments, partly by bribing
the necessary authorities in accordance with accepted
practice, partly by recruiting private armies to pro-
tect their properties from marauders, partly by ap-
pealing to the United States Government for intervention and protection. A decade of this sort of maneu-
vering, during which the oil companies fared spec-
tacularly well, was hardly calculated to put them in
a mood for easy bargaining with the Mexican Government.

For its part, the Mexican officials of the
1920's and 1930's could not take an overly concilia-
tory view to the oil companies even if they wished.
As far as important segments of the Mexican people
were concerned, the Revolution had conquered its
three enemies: the landlords, the Church and the
foreigners. Overt concessions to any of them represented a betrayal of Revolutionary aims.

In this setting, the oil companies allowed
their production to fall off from the 1921 peak.
The drop in production could have been a matter of
deliberate policy; but there is evidence which indi-
cates that the decline must have been due, in part
at any rate, to an unusual run of bad luck. Explora-
tion and drilling activity continued high in the
1920's, but the companies produced an unusual number
of dry holes and uneconomic wells. Throughout the
1920's, as production fell off, the tension and the
pressures grew. There were law suits by the companies aimed at clarifying their titles under the new
Constitution. There were conclaves summoned by government, designed to change concession terms and to
increase tax rates on oil production. As cheap
Venezuelan oil came into production in the late
1920's, and new oil finds appeared within the United
States, the oil companies slackened their explora-
tory efforts in Mexico and allowed their production
to shrink even further.

All the elements for the ultimate confrontation
were now in place. As the Mexican Government saw it,
foreigners controlling the subsoil of Mexico were
not only refusing to make appropriate payments for
the right to export Mexico's precious subsoil resources; they were also damaging the country's economic interests by their arbitrary decisions to
shift their production to more convenient sources.
As the foreign companies saw it, the Mexicans were
making outrageous demands in violation of their
legal obligations and their earlier commitments.

The Great Depression and the advent of Lazaro
Cardenas gave the companies their final reasons for
feeling that they might be on a slippery slide and

that they had nothing to lose by hard bargaining tactics. The signs of this hardening attitude were evident in the continued decline of production and the
increasing use of wasteful exploitation methods in
the oil fields. There appeared to be less and less
resort to practices for maintaining field pressures,
for protecting against fire, for utilizing by-
products effectively, and so on. At the same time,
the tactics of negotiation with unions and government officials grew more and more uninhibited.

There is nothing to suggest that the labor leaders and government officials at this stage did any-
thing to reassure the oil companies concerning the
future. As far as labor was concerned, although the
oil workers' wages were among the very highest in
Mexico and although working conditions were not
notoriously difficult, the demands never ceased. As
for the public officials of the 1930's, they represented a near-revolutionary government in near-
revolutionary times; and they represented that time
and period faithfully. Diego Rivera's caricature
mural in the staircase of the Mexican Presidential
Palace, depicting the greedy and debauched million-
aires of Wall Street, came close to reflecting the
official mood of the times.

It does not matter any longer whether or not
the nationalization of oil might have been avoided.
My own view has always been that the nationalization
was a not-wholly-unexpected nor wholly-unintended
consequence of the uninhibited negotiating tactics
of the oil companies. If the oil companies had
weathered the crises of 1938, they would certainly
have been badgered unmercifully in the years that
followed; in order to raise their taxes from the 15
or 20 percent typical of the 1920's to the 60 percent or so typical of the 1960's, a great deal of
badgering would obviously have been required. Perhaps it was just as well for the long-run position
of other foreign investors in Mexico and for the
growth of the Mexican economy as a whole that the
issue was settled once and for all by the draconian
expropriation of 1938.

The Nationalization of Electric Power

Although the electric power industry, like the
oil industry, finally was nationalized by the Mexican Government, the path toward nationalization and
the factors that impelled the industry along that
path were quite different.

In stressing the differences, one must note at
once that one ingredient indispensable to the outcome in both situations was the same. The Mexican
people took great pleasure and pride from both transactions, as representing in some sense the repossession of mastery in their own house. And that sense
of repossession was all the greater because of the
fundamental importance of the two industries to the
Mexican economy. In practically every other respect,
however, the electric power case seemed the more inevitable, the more natural, of the two situations.

Mexico's electric power era began almost at the
same time as electricity began to appear in the United States and Europe. By the beginning of the twentieth century, electricity was being used as motive
power in a few large mines and was beginning to be
installed for light and power in one or two principal cities. By 1911, electricity was being used
quite widely in the larger mines and factories, and
was illuminating streets and homes in a number of
major cities and towns.

From the first, the Porfirian style of welcome
for the foreigners was very much in evidence. The
four major electrical systems of 1911, for instance,
were all foreign-financed and foreign-run. To be
sure, the foreign investor was not wholly free from
worry over his long-term prospects. For one thing,
even at this early date, Finance Minister Limantour
was already expressing the hope that one day the
equity in these companies might be recaptured by
Mexicans "and never again allowed to depart." For
another thing, complaints about the cost of power
and about the exploitativeness of the companies were
already endemic. But these were small clouds on the
horizon at best. So strong was the general euphoria

of the foreign investors, in fact, that expansion in
the electric power system continued until 1914, four
years after the overthrow of Diaz.

From 1920 to 1929, the installed capacity for
electric power generation in Mexico nearly tripled.
It may be that the extraordinary optimism of the
electric power industry in the United States during
the 1920's carried over in some degree to Mexico.
In any case, foreign investors in electric power had
less reason to worry about the implications of the
Mexican Revolution than investors in mining or oil.
There was little or nothing in the Constitution, after all, to place a cloud on their future rights to
do business in Mexico. Throughout the 1920's, therefore, the foreign power companies expanded. And as
early as 1926, their operations were already heavily
oriented to the "domestic," non-export side of the
economy. By that time, only about one-third of
their power was still being sold to the export-
oriented mines and smelters. Over 45 percent was going to municipalities, homes, and farms, while another 20 percent was going to other types of industry.

It was in this period of their greatest growth,
however, that the first adumbrations of the eventual
nationalization of power companies began to be evident. By 1925, the few power specialists in the
Mexican Government began to campaign for a system of
national rate regulation, along lines which were already commonplace in the United States and Europe.
The reaction of the companies was predictable, perhaps even inevitable, given the time and place.
They resisted every move toward government regulation, not only on the question of rates but also on
such issues as minimum safety regulations and non-
discriminatory rate application. And some of their
arguments--often supported by unassailable facts--
were unavoidably invidious. Whatever the state of
regulation might be in other countries, the companies
claimed, Mexico was in no position to develop and apply a rational and equitable system of public utility
regulation.

By the end of the 1920's, over the protests of

the utility companies, the shadow of a regulatory
system was imposed. The system seems to have been
both corrupt and ineffectual. These traits may have
been proof of the companies' contentions that Mexico
simply did not have the human resources to administer an effective regulatory system; or else, as Mexicans allege, it may have been proof of the utilities'
determination to subvert any such system. More likely, both kinds of factors played a part.

   In any case, the ineffectuality of the system
served as a constant affront to the people of Mexico.
When the Great Depression set in and the public utilities persisted in maintaining their high pre-depres-
sion utility rates, the Mexican people were in no
mood to listen to the companies' explanations in justification of the rates. In any event, the atmos-
phere of the years 1932 and 1933 predisposed the
Mexican nation to receptivity for any radical pro-
posal. It was at this time, therefore, that the
first loud cries for the nationalization of the
power industry were heard.

   In 1933, Mexico's electric power companies introduced the first rate declines in their thirty
years' history. As far as history was concerned,
however, this was a small, irrelevant gesture. Mexico's Sexennial Plan, published in 1934, already was
stating the Revolutionary credo that electric power
was an indispensable condition for industrial and
agricultural growth; it followed, therefore, that
power had to be developed irrespective of prospects
for private profit. This, of course, was a point of
view basically at odds with the private ownership
and development of the electric power industry. In
the end, this was the issue which--more than any
other--pushed the electric power industry into the
hands of the Government.

   Before that final step took place, however, the
industry was to go through a long drawn-out battle
with the Government. Its position in Mexico in the
1930's was not helped by the fact that, while electric power consumption grew rapidly throughout the
latter half of that decade, installed capacity

remained practically unchanged. One could scarcely
blame the utilities for failing to increase their investment. Foreign land and finally foreign oil were
being expropriated all about them; in the circumstances, it would have been impossible for the power
company management, as prudent men, to justify more
investment in Mexico.

Nor can one blame the Mexican people for responding bitterly to the standstill in public utility expansion during the late 1930's. As demand
grew, the usual symptoms of overworked power plants
appeared. Dim-outs and failures developed with increasing frequency. To heap difficulty on difficulty, the outbreak of World War II postponed the day
when the public utilities might reverse their policy.
Mexico limped painfully through the war period,
therefore, beset by problems in the electric power
field.

There is no need to labor too long what followed. When the war ended, the privately-owned utilities were never again allowed to take the initiative in filling Mexico's power needs. Instead, the
Comision Federal de Electricidad, a government entity, took on the task of expanding electric capacity, enlarging its facilities by over one million
kilowatts in the fifteen years after the war. The
expansion undertaken by the private companies during
that period came to only half that amount; and much
of that expansion had to be financed by government-
guaranteed loans.

Once again, however, it is well to realize that
the nationalization of the companies was a consequence of circumstances which neither they nor the
government were free to do very much about.

By World War II, it is clear, the Government
could not afford to behave openhandedly toward the
foreign companies. Given the limping performance of
the companies from the 1920's on, the issue had become too loaded emotionally to permit the Government
to put itself in the light of aider and abettor of
the foreigners. Rate hikes commensurate with the

general price rise, for instance, were out of the
question.

There were other means, however, by which the
Government could avoid grinding the companies between the millstones of rising costs and unchanging
rates. One of these was for the Government quietly
to sell power to the electric companies at wholesale
rates, for redistribution by the companies to consumers; another means was to help the companies finance such expansion in their systems as they were
willing to undertake; a third means was to tolerate
substandard performance by the companies in the delivery of electrical current. All of these means
were used to ease the companies' lot.

But these palliatives did little to change the
basic situation. Clearly, there was no prospect of
growth and profit for private utilities in Mexico.
In the latter 1950's, the companies began to think
of selling out. Soon thereafter, at an intricate
juncture in the political situation in Mexican life,
the Government saw an advantage in buying out the
companies. A half-willing seller and an eager buyer
are all that are needed to consummate a sale. On
September 1, 1960, amidst mutual exchanges of con-
gratulations by the companies and the Government,
the country was resplendent with posters which read:

LAND	-	1910
OIL	-	1938
ELECTRIC POWER	-	1960

THE NEW INVESTOR

Although the electric power industry was not
nationalized until 1960, it represented the final
liquidation of an era which had really begun to
close many years earlier. With the end of World War
II, the flow of foreign direct investment into Mexico
had developed a different emphasis. By that time,
foreign investors had begun to show a strong interest
in manufacturing facilities to serve the Mexican market.

This interest was not wholly new. The Ford
Motor Company had set up an assembly plant in Mexico
as early as 1925, and other American manufacturing
enterprises had appeared even earlier. But the
Great Depression and the 1938 oil expropriations had
soured the investor's taste for investment in Mexico.
Eventually, however, the long period of Mexico's
growth from the end of the Great Depression to the
close of World War II made it a much more interesting target for United States producers; and President Aleman's policies of high tariffs plus import
licensing after World War II provided the necessary
spur for many exporters to take the leap by setting
up production facilities inside the country. By the
latter 1950's, United States-owned subsidiaries had
come to account for about one-sixth of Mexico's manufacturing output. Since these subsidiaries were on
the whole among the larger firms in the country,
they seemed to the casual observer to dominate Mexican industrial life.

Mexicans have debated the economic consequences
of this great wave of investment with considerable
passion. The debate has ranged widely over many
questions. Were these foreign investors "decapitalizing" Mexico, that is, draining off more money than
they were bringing into the country? Were they chok-
ing off Mexican business initiative by driving small
business to the wall and absorbing the best talent
into foreign-owned firms? Were they making Mexico
especially vulnerable to sudden industrial disaster,
which might develop if the foreigners chose at some
stage to withdraw from the country? Were they block-
ing the further industrialization of Mexico by refusing to buy their industrial materials and technical
needs from the Mexican economy?

The argument that foreign investment has been
bad for the Mexican balance-of-payments has had a
strong impact on Mexican thinking. Mexicans have
noted that the flow of dividends, interest, and royalty payments to foreign investors in any year has
usually outweighed the flow of fresh capital into
Mexico. Accordingly, the foreign companies have
been seen as "decapitalizing" the Mexican economy.

The full balance-of-payments effects of these
investments, of course, have been very much more complicated. Apart from affecting the flow of capital
and service payments, investors have had other effects in Mexican payments. They have contributed to
the great wave of import-replacement which has characterized Mexico during the past two decades, thereby presumably saving foreign exchange. They have
been responsible in some measure for the increase in
exports of manufactured products from Mexico during
the same period. Just to complicate matters further,
however, these enterprises also have been responsible
for some of the increase in Mexico's demand for capital goods and industrial materials, thus throwing
new strains on the Mexican balance of payments. And,
finally, insofar as these foreign investments increased Mexico's real income, they also have increased the aggregate demand of Mexican consumers
for foreign goods.

Any efforts to balance out factors such as
these are inevitably an exercise in conjecture. One
or two systematic efforts at measuring the full
balance-of-payments effects of the facilities in Mexico seem to suggest that they were more than earning
their way in balance-of-payment terms; one such study,
in fact, suggests a net balance-of-payment contribution on the order of $450 millions annually. These
conjectures tend to be supported by the fact that,
contrary to the usual assumption in Mexico, foreigners
seem to have integrated their facilities very deeply
into the Mexican economy. In 1957, for example, United States-owned manufacturing subsidiaries in Mexico
imported directly only $83 million of the $406 million
in materials which they purchased in that year. (A
notable exception to the pattern was the automobile
industry, which tended to import the great majority
of its materials from abroad until forced by the Mexican Government to change its policies in the early
1960's.)

The foreign manufacturing firms in Mexico often
exhibited a heavy-handedness in their relations with
the Mexican public which was calculated to do them no
good in the long run. There were times, for instance,

when the foreign community seemed to be placing itself in the position of resisting Mexican tax reforms. At the same time, however, these firms tended to set high standards by Mexican norms in such
important areas as the payment of taxes, the adher-
ence to labor agreements, the institution of in-
service training, and so on. This generally salutary line of conduct may have been stimulated by a
sense of what was necessary for survival; but, whatever the motivations, the performance helped provide
constructive norms for Mexico's industrial class as
a whole.

Confronted with a great flow of industrial investment coming principally from the United States,
the reaction of a succession of Mexican administra-
tions has been understandingly ambivalent. On the
one hand, no president of Mexico could afford to em-
brace the presence of the foreign investor, given
the Revolutionary symbolism of Mexico; on the other
hand, this particular breed of investor was obviously being helpful to the Mexican economy in a number
of different ways: in helping to tide over the
short-term pressures on the Mexican balance of payments; in helping to meet the challenge of the import replacement program which Mexico so badly wished
to achieve; and, in bringing technology of an advanced kind into the Mexican economy.

The result of the official ambivalence has been
to provide a succession of responses from the Mexican political institutions which could hardly be
called consistent in their approach.

The first manifestation of this wavering pattern involved presidents Avila Camacho and Aleman.
In the early 1940's, President Avila Camacho was responsible for the enactment of legislation which em-
powered the Mexican Government to designate industries in which foreign investors would be prohibited
from holding a controlling interest. A few years
later, President Aleman was responsible for imple-
menting the legislation with a listing of industries
which had no significant restrictive effect, such as
the bottling of orange drinks and radio broadcasting.

For a time it appeared that Aleman's successor,
Ruiz Cortines, would place added restraints upon the
inflow of foreign investment. But when the peso ran
into difficulties in the middle 1950's, the response
of Ruiz Cortines was to welcome such investment with
an open hand.

If any Mexican president followed a clear line
with respect to the foreign investor, it was President Lopez Mateos, the successor to Ruiz Cortines.
By a number of different administrative techniques,
Lopez Mateos made it clear that he expected foreign
investors to toe the mark. Among other things, he
put pressure on investors to take Mexican industrialists into partnership; to buy more of their supplies
from Mexican sources; to avoid the use of imported
technical and executive personnel; and so on. But
there was a certain basic pragmatism in his approach,
just as there was an underlying pragmatism in the approach of some of the investors who confronted him.
How else could one explain the extraordinary marriage
represented by a joint undertaking between Dupont
(the epitome of foreign capitalism) and Pemex (the
quintessence of naturalized enterprise)?

The pressures of the Lopez Mateos regime also
varied with the state of health of the Mexican peso
and the state of balance of internal Mexican politics.
As a result, Lopez Mateos was far more insistent in
his demands in the years from 1960 to 1962 than in
the last two years of his regime.

Still, one could discern a certain consistency
in government pressures, which stands as an omen of
future policy. One such line of pressures relates
to the mining and extractive industries. For example, Lopez Mateos secured the enactment of a statute
which, in effect, forgave mining companies to the extent of 50 percent of their tax liabilities, provided
that the ownership of such companies was at least 50
percent Mexican. In addition, the Mexican Government
in 1965 imposed severe import restrictions upon
foreign-owned sulphur companies which were exporting
the product in large quantities to the United States.

It is perfectly clear that non-replenishable
raw materials are looked upon in the Mexican economy
in a special light. In this field, the foreign investor has to take on a special burden. He has to
live with the memories of less inhibited times, when
mining companies and petroleum companies were "exploiting" the Mexican economy, at least by present-
day standards. He has also to live with the emotional burden that goes with the uncontrolled shipment
by foreigners of non-replenishable resources. It
would take an uninhibited optimist to assume that investment in export-oriented enterprises involving
the exploitation of this kind of raw material will
have easy going in Mexico's future.

In projecting the future for the foreign investor in Mexico, however, one must also take into account other factors of an even more general nature.
One of these general factors is the changing attitude of the private sector in Mexico.

Two decades ago, one could have discerned some
sharp and important distinctions in the reactions of
the different private groups within the Mexican economy. One such group, known as CONCANACO, was a
national organization composed principally of local
chambers merchants and traders. A second group, con-
sisting principally of the larger industrialists of
the country, went under the general identification
of CONCAMIN. And, within the structure of CONCAMIN,
there was a separate maverick group, composed of
many smaller manufacturing firms, which we shall
identify here as CNIT.

A decade or two ago, CONCANACO seemed to see
its interests as being parallel in many respects
with those of the foreign investors. Engaged in import and export trade and related in various ways to
the major foreign interests of the country, this
group was at first unequivocal in its support of unrestricted foreign trade and uninhibited foreign investment.

The CONCAMIN, on the other hand, represented the
larger firms in the industrial community of Mexico.

While many Mexicans in this group also had close
ties to foreign enterprises, they began to see that
community of interest, a decade or two ago, in
rather different terms. Their concern was to have
heavy protection against competing imports, an easy
flow of credit, and freedom from governmental inter-
ference.

But CNIT, purporting to represent a much larger
number of small producers in the Mexican economy,
took a very different line. This group, taking the
role of the Revolutionary conscience of Mexico, ham-
mered mercilessly at the local representatives of
the giant foreign "trusts" which seemed to be taking
over the Mexican economy. Using the style and seman-
tics of the anti-gringo nationalists, the CNIT took
the foreign investors to task on all the questions
which their presence in Mexico had raised.

As the years passed, however, one could detect
a clear convergence of view among the three industrial groups. The CONCANACO, once devoted to free
trade and easy foreign investment, came in the course
of time to see its interests as being much less related to foreign commerce and much more related to
the internal markets of Mexico. This was a natural
evolution, reflecting in good measure the growing
importance of Mexico's internal markets.

The development may also have reflected the
fact that by the 1960's, interests of Mexico's old
commercial groups had broadened out considerably.
By then, the principal groups had diversified their
interests over the spectrum of industrial and commercial activities, from banking on the one hand to
manufacturing and wholesale trade on the other. As
a result, the line between CONCANACO and CONCAMIN
had broken down somewhat. Now both were prepared to
accept the need for infant industry protection; both
were prepared to see the usefulness of government investment, provided that the investment did not impinge too strongly upon areas which they felt confi-
dent to handle without foreign help; and where foreigners did impinge on such areas, both were prepared
to propose that the role of the outsiders should be
curtailed and restrained.

As the years went on, the industrial populists of the CNIT also began to show some signs of change. Some of their outstanding leaders, in the course of time, began to demonstrate that good propagandists can also make good businessmen. Success turned a few of their leading firms into relatively large enterprises. As they achieved growth, they also achieved a certain restraint in expression and a certain balance of view which narrowed the distinctions between themselves and the CONCAMIN group.

By the mid-1960's, many differences among the various business groups still remained. But there was one view they tended to share. This was the view that in some circumstances--the circumstances were somewhat differently defined by the different groups--foreign investment could be harmful to the proper development of the Mexican economy. In those cases, it was clear, restraint upon foreigners was justified. In other situations, however, the foreigners' contribution to Mexican growth would be warmly welcomed.

From the United States side of the border most of the recent developments in Mexico have tended to be seen through rose-colored spectacles: indeed, the picture of Mexico in the mid-1960's as seen by prospective U.S. investors was one of nearly unbounded enthusiasm. After forty years of political stability and almost as many years of economic growth, United States investors had come to see Mexico as an exemplary neighbor, a splendid market, and an outstanding area for investment. The nationalization of oil had long since faded out of the United States memory; the Mexican nationalization of the utilities had been accepted by the United States public as a fair and amicable arrangement; the Mexican discrimination against foreign-owned mining companies had been taken in stride; and the ad hoc pressures on foreign companies to admit local partners, buy local materials, and hire local technicians, had been accepted as the proper price for admission to a large and lucrative market.

One could hardly quarrel with such an evaluation;

Mexico had certainly earned it. If there was any-
thing troublesome about the net judgment of United
States investors, it was not so much the judgment
itself as the degree of assurance with which it was
held. While some investors had reached this conclusion soberly and guardedly, most seemed to have
leaped to the conclusion without much real consideration of the severe limits of tolerance within which
foreign investors operated in the Mexican economy.
As a people, the Mexicans of the 1960's showed a
strong sense of national purpose and national self-
assurance. The fruits of their economic triumphs
were almost within their grasp, and they had no desire or intention of sharing any more of those
fruits than was necessary. They were prepared to
accept the support of foreign investors, as long as
it was clear that the support was necessary or desirable. They were not prepared to tolerate that
support when the net effects were more ambiguous.

     If the remaining area of mutual interests be-
tween Mexico and its foreign investors were small or
were shrinking fast, one would be inclined to see
trouble ahead. The area, however, is still large.
If there are grounds for uneasiness, they stem from
the fact that some foreign investors seem unaware
that the area of mutual interest has its limits and
that the limits, in time, may shrink. When that
happens, a foreign investor without a proper sense
of history may feel somehow betrayed, while a Mexican steeped in his concept of history will wonder at
the reaction. The awakening is always ruder when
the dreams have been sweet.

BENJAMIN LOGAN

CHARLES GANO TALBERT

Benjamin Logan

Kentucky Frontiersman

UNIVERSITY OF KENTUCKY PRESS

TO DOROTHY JARETT TALBERT